ONCE UPON A TIME IN THE WEST

Once upon a Time in the West
*Essays on the Politics of Thought
and Imagination*

Jan Zwicky

McGILL-QUEEN'S UNIVERSITY PRESS
Montreal & Kingston · London · Chicago

© McGill-Queen's University Press 2023

ISBN 978-0-2280-1708-0 (cloth)
ISBN 978-0-2280-1709-7 (paper)
ISBN 978-0-2280-1829-2 (ePDF)
ISBN 978-0-2280-1830-8 (ePUB)

Legal deposit second quarter 2023
Bibliothèque nationale du Québec

Printed in Canada on acid-free paper that is 100% ancient forest free (100% post-consumer recycled), processed chlorine free

This book has been published with the help of a grant from the Canadian Federation for the Humanities and Social Sciences, through the Awards to Scholarly Publications Program, using funds provided by the Social Sciences and Humanities Research Council of Canada.

  Canada Council for the Arts   Conseil des Arts du Canada

We acknowledge the support of the Canada Council for the Arts.
Nous remercions le Conseil des arts du Canada de son soutien.

Library and Archives Canada Cataloguing in Publication

Title: Once upon a time in the West : essays on the politics of thought and imagination / Jan Zwicky
Names: Zwicky, Jan, 1955– author.
Description: Includes bibliographical references and index.
Identifiers: Canadiana (print) 20220496978 | Canadiana (ebook) 20220497028 | ISBN 9780228017080 (cloth) | ISBN 9780228017097 (paper) | ISBN 9780228018308 (ePUB) | ISBN 9780228018292 (ePDF)
Subjects: LCSH: Philosophy. | LCSH: Knowledge, Theory of. | LCSH: Civilization, Western—21st century—Philosophy.
Classification: LCC B21 .Z856 2023 | DDC 191—dc23

The text face is Requiem, designed by Jonathan Hoefler. Titles, captions, and tables are set in Carol Twombly's Chaparral.

Contents

vii   Preface

3   Auden as Philosopher: How Poets Think

21   Wilderness and Agriculture

29   Once upon a Time in the West: Heidegger and the Poets

39   Lyric Realism: Nature Poetry, Silence, and Ontology

47   The Ethics of the Negative Review

59   Integrity and Ornament

71   The Novels of Pascal: A Review of *Correction* by Thomas Bernhard

85   Being Will Be Here, Beauty Will Be Here, But This Beauty That Visits Us Now Will Be Gone

95   A Note on Jane Jacobs's *Systems of Survival,* or Why We Will Not Be Able to Prevent Global Ecological Collapse

103   On Rules and Moral Beauty

109   Lyric, Narrative, Memory

117   The Syntax of Ethical Style

135   Frost and Snow

147   Haydn's F-Flat

151   Acknowledgements

153   Notes

165   References

179   Index

Preface

Western civilization is over. By that I mean the culture that replaced the European Middle Ages, that began with the Renaissance, saw the invention of the printing press and the telescope, fostered the Reformation, the Scientific Revolution, the Enlightenment, engendered capitalism and a host of European empires, persevered through the Romantic Reaction, and went on in the twentieth century to dominate global economic policy and social aspiration, is finished. The signs are everywhere: teetering economies, democratic institutions under threat, belligerent populism on the rise, ecological cataclysm on the horizon. Those on the receiving end of the West's imperial aggressions have questioned the appropriateness of the term 'civilization.' But violence is endemic to the human species. Males are territorial: they fight males of other tribes; and they fight males of their own tribes in bids for status. They constrain females in both overt and subtle ways. If 'civilization' means a culture in which aggression and atrocity are absent, then the planet has never seen a human version.

I am not interested in the proximate causes of this cultural demise — automation, the global shift to digital technologies, addiction to life online, the decline of literacy, the evisceration of humanistic studies, the growing gap between the less-than-one-percent and everyone else, human overpopulation conjoined with accelerating rates of diet-induced human disease. What holds my attention is the root cause of these various immediate crises, the headwaters of the river that forms the delta. At the source of many of the West's problems is a *way of thinking* that is also responsible for some of its most signal achievements. This way of thinking had its genesis roughly six hundred years ago: European absorption of Islamic learning in mathematics and astronomy merged with imperial enterprise to precipitate mechanized industry at home and predatory resource extraction abroad. These in turn fostered the growth of capitalism, the military-industrial complex, and Big Technology. Despite its self-image as 'objective,' the West's style of thought is not politically neutral: it is intensely anthropocentric; it has led those who adopt it to regard the extra-human world as nothing more than timber licenses and drilling sites; it cannot recognize value unless it is monetized; it is oblivious to context and has trouble seeing big pictures; while it analyzes, mechanizes, digitizes, and systematizes, it rejects empathy and compassion as 'distorting influences' and insists that blustery defensiveness over turf is compatible with intellectual probity.

Philosophers call ways of thinking *epistemologies*: views about how we know what we know. Epistemologies are traditionally allied with metaphysics: views about what exists, what there is to be known. This book looks at how the West's dominant epistemology has produced critical blindnesses about reality, blindnesses whose terrifying consequences even now begin to unfold.

In many of the essays that follow, I describe and discuss an alternative way of thinking that I call lyric. Over the millennia, lyric attention has been practised by many human beings — in the West, most have been artists, naturalists, or religious — but since the seventeenth century, lyric thought has been increasingly derogated in European and Euro-colonial cultures. I focus on it not because it represents a solution to our problems — I do not think solutions exist — but because it provides a foil against which the nature of resourcist thinking reveals itself even more starkly. Historically, in some cultures, lyric awareness has balanced resourcist thinking. Now that the West's unbalanced style is global, the threat posed by that style is global, too.

Not all these essays address this theme directly. "The Ethics of the Negative Review," "Integrity and Ornament," "Rules and Moral Beauty," and "The Novels of Pascal" speak to particular manifestations of the mental cast of the resourcist juggernaut: its scorning of empathy, its inability to embody integrity, its insistence on explicit and exhaustive criteria of evaluation, and its perennial struggle with skepticism about meaning.

Because I do not think solutions are available, my aim is simply to understand how we got here. Not to make a map of the local streets and alleyways, but to grasp the nature of the means of transport that gave those streets and alleyways their inevitable form. The point is to go down with our eyes open. Or, as an old Greek book used to recommend, to know ourselves.

Notes and references are provided but, in an effort to keep the discussion readable, they are not marked in the text. Readers interested in the details will find them, cued to page number and phrase or name, at the back of the book. Where the reference is general in nature and both the author and title are mentioned in the text, I have not added a note: complete bibliographic information can be found in the list of references. Unless otherwise indicated, translations are mine.

JZ
Heriot Ridge · 21 August 2021

ONCE UPON A TIME IN THE WEST

Auden as Philosopher:
How Poets Think

In the final section of "Making, Knowing and Judging," his inaugural lecture as Professor of Poetry at Oxford in 1956, W.H. Auden offers what he calls his theory of poetry. He describes it as a personal account, a private profession of faith. But it's significantly more than that. It is, in fact, an account of how Auden, as poet, *knows what he knows* — in other words, it's an epistemology. I agree that aspects of what Auden has to say reflect his personal temperament and preoccupations; but in many respects, it's a fine account of lyric comprehension in general. Its basic lineaments are ones that many other poets and artists would recognize. And I'd like to suggest that Auden, as lyric epistemologist, presents us with a deep and cogent challenge to the picture of knowing that currently dominates global resourcist culture.

At the core of Auden's theory is the faculty of imagination. This may seem immediately to contradict any claim that Auden could be offering an account of how anyone, even a poet, knows. "The imagination makes things up!" it will be objected. "It can't possibly provide us with *knowledge* of anything!" But if we reflect a moment, we will realize that there are several senses of the word 'imagination' and not all of them mean the same thing. There is the 'making things up' sense, certainly; but there is also something we could call 'thinking in images' — the sort of thing a carpenter does when she's building something, or that a tailor does when he's putting a shirt together, or what any of us do when we're trying to follow IKEA assembly instructions.

At the core of thinking in images is what Ludwig Wittgenstein called 'seeing as' — being able to see one thing *as* another. We also do it, even more strongly, when we see the duck *as* a rabbit or the rabbit *as* a duck in figure 1 on the following page. Or when we see the Necker cube first projecting down and to the right, and then up

Figure 1: *Duck-rabbit*

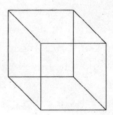

Figure 2: *Necker cube*

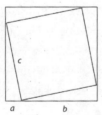 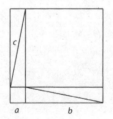

Figure 3: *Proof of Pythagorean theorem,*
$a^2 + b^2 = c^2$

and to the left, in figure 2. And, as Max Wertheimer pointed out, such 'seeing as' is basic to grasping visual proofs in geometry — for example, the demonstration of the Pythagorean theorem in figure 3.

Wertheimer also stressed the importance of 'hearing as' for our comprehension of melody. Notice that it doesn't matter in what key someone hums "Row, row, row your boat" — we recognize the tune whether it's sung in G major or D-flat. This suggests that a melody is a kind of aural 'shape,' which we identify *as a whole* regardless of the pitch values of individual notes, and even when some of those individual notes are wrong. 'Seeing as' is also at the root of our ability to understand powerful metaphors and to recognize them as powerful: "The kingfisher chortles / and falls like an axe through a hole in the rain." This kind of imagination, then, is an important way in which we learn about aspects of the world. Thinking in images, far from making things up, actually helps us perceive what is right in front of our eyes.

This sense, interestingly, connects with the oldest roots of the word: the etymology of 'imagination' ultimately leads us back to a Greek word that means *to bring to light*. This is at the core of what Auden means when he says that it is *through* imagination that the poet knows the world. The objects of the imagination, he tells us, are "encountered," they *oblige* us to respond; if a thing does not oblige the imagination to respond, it is *not known*. He is pointedly not saying that the imagination makes things up, or embellishes them, or that it fantasizes or otherwise retreats from reality. He is saying that the imagination *perceives things that exist.*

~

But this isn't all he says.

Auden's poetic epistemology has four components: an account of what he calls the Primary Imagination; an account of what he calls the Secondary Imagination; a discussion of the origin of the work of art; and, as a prelude, his evidence that we should believe it. (I am inverting the order here because I think his evidence is more clearly evidence once one knows what the view is.)

The terms 'Primary Imagination' and 'Secondary Imagination,' he says, are borrowed from Coleridge; and there are indeed Coleridgian echoes in the way Auden deploys them. But there is also an important difference: Coleridge's account is deeply and explicitly indebted to Kant, while Auden's steers well clear of Idealist metaphysics. The two accounts coincide primarily in the idea that the imagination reveals to us deep truths about the world.

The Primary Imagination, according to Auden, perceives sacred beings and sacred events. These are the things it knows. (Auden is fully aware that many people don't believe such things exist — we'll come to his discussion of this problem in a moment.) When it perceives a sacred being or event, Auden says, the Primary Imagination must respond with "a passion of awe." The awe may vary in intensity, and may range "from joyous wonder to panic dread." Sacred beings are themselves various: they may be beautiful or ugly, beatific or grotesque. Also, Primary Imaginations differ: they don't all recognize the same sacred beings or events. Nonetheless, "every imagination responds to those it recognizes in the same way." And there are *some* sacred beings that seem to be "sacred to all imaginations": Auden lists the moon, fire, snakes, darkness, silence, nothing, and death.

In a subsidiary remark, we are told that "[t]he realm of the Primary Imagination is without freedom, sense of time or humour." What does he mean by "without freedom"? —That there is no possibility of choice: in the presence of a sacred being or event, the Primary Imagination *must* respond, and can respond only with awe. This remark, then, echoes other key claims in the section as a whole: that it is poetry's duty to praise, and the poet's duty to be grateful; and that the Primary Imagination is not 'active.' It is a faculty of receptive knowing and 'does' nothing. It *desires* nothing except to praise.

Auden's claim that the Primary Imagination has no sense of time and his later remark that it is "self-forgetful" together constitute striking echoes of what Freud in his metapsychological works calls "primary process." This is the mode of awareness that, according to Freud, operates in dreams, in slips of the tongue, in prelinguistic children. It is characterized by timelessness, by the absence of a sense of self, by nonlogical associative relationships, and it often resists verbal formulation. Charles Rycroft, one of Freud's most penetrating commentators, has linked it directly to the activity of creative artists. Auden, as a number of his reviews and his famous elegy attest, had read Freud; and Freud, if he had not read Coleridge, would certainly have read Kant, as well as Schelling and Schiller, who were also influences on Coleridge. But Auden, in his 'theory of poetry,' is clearly giving an account of his own experience, and Freud, in *The Interpretation of Dreams* and "The Unconscious," is just as clearly giving a summary of his clinical (and perhaps also personal) experience. That is: although the echoes between the two are significant, and we have reason to suspect that Auden's choice of terms may have been reinforced by his reading of Freud, it nonetheless appears that the two accounts constitute mutually reinforcing reports from two independent witnesses. The third component of Auden's characterization — that the "realm of the Primary Imagination is without ... humour" — may seem to undercut a comparison with Freud, since Freud also located the source of many jokes in the primary-process activity of the unconscious. However, what I suspect Auden means is that the Primary Imagination's gaze is often chillingly impersonal: the gods laugh, but not at things that humans find funny. As Graham Greene remarked, there's a splinter of ice in a writer's heart. With this observation, I think Freud would concur.

The Secondary Imagination, by contrast, is active. It aims to discern *fitting* means of expression for the awe delivered up to it by the Primary Imagination. It attends, Auden says, "not [to] the sacred and the profane, but [to] the beautiful and ugly." Unlike the Primary Imagination, the Secondary Imagination is articulate: it can discuss, dispute, and *figure out* how to make things beautiful. (Again, there is an interesting echo of what Freud termed "secondary process." In Freud, the hallmark of secondary process is language-use, which discriminates and preserves logical orders in thought.) Auden believes we all recognize that there is no point arguing about whether something is sacred — either you see it or you don't — but he is confident that if one of us thinks a form is *beautiful* and the other thinks it isn't, "we cannot both help agreeing that one of us must be wrong."

In this, surely, Auden himself is just wrong. Many people believe that, as the saying goes, beauty is in the eye of the beholder. Perhaps Auden lived among a cabal of Platonists; but this is unlikely. The remark may have its root in the final feature Auden ascribes to the Secondary Imagination: he says that it is social, more specifically that it "craves agreement with other minds." It has, he suggests, "a bourgeois nature. It approves of regularity, of spatial symmetry and temporal repetition, of law and order: it disapproves of loose ends, irrelevance and mess." Could this be what Auden means by 'beauty'? It's true that there's a good chance that two observers, however divergent their tastes, will be able to agree about whether something is symmetrical or not, or whether it's characterized by a little, a lot, or no, mess. But to say that beauty amounts to nothing more than symmetry and tidiness is indeed to announce one's outlook as bourgeois; it reduces beauty to a safe, unchallenging prettiness. The idea that that's what we mean when we describe Yexyexéscen (Mount Robson) or Donatello's *Penitent Magdalene* as beautiful is, at best, unintuitive.

In other words, a number of the details offered here tell us less about the Secondary Imagination than they do about Auden's temperament — which was unabashedly Victorian. I will have more to say about this when we come to compare Auden's account with the accounts of other poets. For the moment, I'd like to underline two remarks that appear to hold, independently of Auden's Victorian sensibility: first, that the Secondary Imagination is concerned with finding a fitting or *appropriate* expression of the Primary Imagination's awe; and second, that it "craves agreement with other minds." Fitting expression need not be beautiful; what it must do is *compel*. And if what has aroused one's awe is something outrageous or appalling, the most compelling expression may be a snarl of rage, or a sob of grief. Of course, if one lives in an extremely reserved or repressed culture, the most compelling gesture may well be a taut ironic quatrain. But what this shows is that 'fittingness,' appropriateness, is always a negotiation between private vision and public intelligibility. This is the burden, I believe, of the suggestion regarding agreement with other minds: if an artistic gesture is to reach a wide audience, that gesture must be couched in terms a wide audience can read. In other words: whatever they or we may believe about the nature of the beautiful, artists, if they wish to go public, are still faced with the task of *communication*. Perhaps they don't all "*crave* agreement with other minds"; but Auden is right this far: if you go to the trouble of publishing, it's pretty clear that you wish to be understood. Thus I believe we may summarize Auden's view in the following, slightly more general, terms:

The passive awe of the Primary Imagination precipitates a desire to express that awe; the Secondary Imagination says that the expression must be both true to the experience and, if possible, intelligible to others; and it works to make it so. This is the origin of the work of art. According to Auden, because the origin involves "the inspiration of sacred awe," its adequate expression requires a rite. The poem reveals its ritual nature in its "deliberately and ostentatiously different" use of language. "Even when it employs the diction and rhythms of conversation, it employs them as a deliberate informality, presupposing the norm with which they are intended to contrast."

As Western European and other cultures disintegrate under the pressure of globalized commerce, the cultural norms of which Auden speaks are eroded. Many writers and readers would not now recognize what he is referring to. Does this mean that his claim about the ritual nature of poetic utterance merely reflects his own Victorian and Anglican temperament? Perhaps, or perhaps in part, although we see in many other cultures a stress on the particular and peculiar vocabulary of what each has called poetry. Auden's claim then might also mean that what is written or spoken in a cultural vacuum cannot *be* poetry, cannot serve poetry's function. That is: culturally recognized norms of language-use, from which lyric utterance can be distinguished, are essential if language is to point successfully to primary-process awareness of the world. This is a broad claim, too broad for us to explore here, but well worth consideration.

What is the evidence that Auden's fundamental claims about the experience of awe and the desire to communicate it correctly capture how poets think and experience the world? Auden's defence is interestingly anthropological. And it is here that he allows that many in his own culture will react negatively to talk of the sacred. He points to the fact that in cultures that do acknowledge a social distinction between the sacred and the profane, poets have a public role, and poetry itself is either public or esoteric. In cultures that don't make this distinction, like the West's, the poet has no public role: she functions as an amateur, and poetry is "intimate." Typically generous, Auden is not out to deride the times. His point is simply this: *whether or not* a culture values the sacred or recognizes that it is distinct from the profane, it recognizes that the poet's vocation is directed towards it. In cultures that value the sacred, the poet is held in high regard; in cultures that disparage the sacred, the poet, too, is disparaged or marginalized.

It's like someone who we think is crazy saying: "I'm aware you think I'm crazy, and I'm aware *why* you think I'm crazy. Indeed, I can give you a panoramic view of your reasons." This sort of gesture may not alleviate our distaste; but it must give us pause. If he knows that his vocation must marginalize him, why would such an obviously intelligent and gifted man stick with it? Why didn't he become an investment banker? But even if Auden is sane enough to realize he must *sound* crazy to us, two large questions remain: (1) Is this a widespread phenomenon? Do other poets think this way, too? And (2), even supposing the answer to (1) is 'yes,' can the way poets think be of any real interest to those of us living in the outwash of what we have called Western culture?

～

The answer to the first question is indeed *yes*: I believe many poets from many cultures would recognize awe and its fitting expression as hallmarks of their vocation. I myself recognize core aspects of my own practice in what Auden says — though, of course, as a person of no orthodox religious affiliation, raised by atheists in a secular culture, I, too, shy away from using the word 'sacred.' In its place, I tend to use the word 'ontological' — a nice, recondite

Greek polysyllable which is acceptable in academic philosophical circles while remaining likely to catch the attention of those who reflect on — let's call them 'spiritual' — matters from positions outside such circles. More briefly, and defensiveness aside: I believe that what Auden means by 'sacredness' is what I mean by 'being'; and that he intends to point, as I do, to our astonishment before what-is, our sense of its extraordinary power, its overwhelming *meaning*. The languages of commerce and technology, of cost-benefit analysis and systematic reductionism, can get no purchase on an experience of this sort.

Here are some other testimonies to this effect. I have deliberately chosen contemporary Canadian examples, but many non-Canadians — Jane Hirshfield, Robert Gray, Li-Young Lee — also spring to mind.

ROBERT BRINGHURST: *I don't know how poetry knows. What it knows I also cannot say, though I have heard poetry say it.... That it knows seems to me only a kind of tautology poorly phrased. I would rather say that poetry is one among the many forms of knowing, and maybe it is knowing in the purest form we know. I would rather say that knowing freed from the agenda of possession and control — knowing in the sense of stepping in tune with being, hearing and echoing the music and heartbeat of being — is what we mean by poetry.... What poetry knows, or what it strives to know, is the dancing at the heart of being.*

DON DOMANSKI: *... poetry and the sacred[:] ... For me, there's an intimate connection between the two, so intimate in fact that I can't really separate them out.... There's an umbilical point somewhere that nurtures both, like twins fed from the same source. By sacred, I don't necessarily mean religious, or spiritual in the New Age sense of that word.... I mean how each thing holds a mystery, simply because it exists, because existence itself is sacred.... Poetry helps to enhance and deepen our experience of existence, not just by the use of words, but by the fact that despite their use something else is carried along with them.*

At the heart of poetry is a pre-verbal reality....

...Deepening our lives essentially means to be aware, to answer the call from life itself, to practise the veneration of its numerous forms. This has nothing to

do with religion, per se; rather, religion and art grow out of this veneration....
[H]uman beings... have this irresistible urge to acknowledge the awe they feel in the presence of creation.

An atheist can feel that as deeply as a believer, the magnitude of the experience can be exactly the same in either case. No amount of negation can push aside this longing for reverence, it wells up, regardless, in every human being.

RALPH GUSTAFSON: *The constancy of surprise and wonder marks poetry, surprise that reality includes its own meaning, wonder that the significant discovery has not been known before.... We have come to call the [discovery of endowed reality] by such names as inspiration, divination, rapture. The names are old-fashioned to us; they partly do well enough, the deepness of living is contained in the indications. The trouble with them is that they are not accurate enough; they imply the leaving hold of reality, the supersession of desire over fact, they imply frenzy, superstition. A sober ecstasy is required. Poetry is real, it is what is....*

[T]he formalities of [making poetry] are attuned by the conscious will, the ambition not to destroy, the joy of mastering the material of words — but, in the first instance, in a combination of sensitivity and experience, of illuminated shaping, the poet is not made but given to....

DENNIS LEE: *... voice embodies being... if [a voice] rings true, you sense it resonating with things on that wavelength across the whole breadth of what is.... A meditative poem does its job when the vocal shifts... enact a trajectory.... And if you're lucky, [that trajectory] enacts an ontophony, a music of being.... On a good day it just resonates in things. It's there to be heard.*

TIM LILBURN: *Around everything is an epidermis of narrative, a layer of hypotheses, orders, causal grids by which the world is rendered intelligible. Poetry's fundamental appetite is ecstatic; its curiosity yearns beyond this barrier of intelligibility to know the withinness of things.*

The knowledge poetry seeks is the most intimate, the names it aspires to utter [are] those which its subjects... would intone if they stood to sing.... Poetry leans into the world and back to [a] state when the mind bespoke the souls of things....

DON MCKAY: *... before, under, and through the wonderful terrible wrestling with words and music there is a state of mind which I'm calling 'poetic attention'....*

[I]t's a sort of readiness, a species of longing which is without the desire to possess, and it does not really wish to be talked about. To me, this is a form of knowing which counters the 'primordial grasp' in home-making, and celebrates the wilderness of the other; it gives ontological applause.

ANNE MICHAELS: A poem can give us night vision; getting used to the dark, we begin to make things out. The invisible rendered visible: breath on glass.

P.K. PAGE: I am a two-dimensional being. I live in a sheet of paper.... The tines of a fork pushed vertically through the paper appear as four thin silver ellipses. I may, in a moment of insight, realize that it is more than coincidence that four identical but independent silver rings have entered my world. In a further breakthrough I may glimpse their unity, even sense the entire fork — large, glimmering, extraordinary. Just beyond my sight. Mystifying; marvellous.

My two-dimensional consciousness yearns to catch some overtone which will convey that great resonant silver object.... [I]n all essential particulars writing and painting are interchangeable. They are alternate roads to silence.

SUE SINCLAIR: ... epiphany is what I go to poetry for. It's the heart of the matter for me.... By epiphany I mean a sudden moment of insight, a sense of revelation[,] ... the new insight bringing with it a kind of wonder or awe.... The term's historical usage continues to resonate in its secular incarnation, ... for even the secular epiphany carries with it a sense of being opened up to something greater than myself, divine or otherwise.... James Joyce, in an early draft of Portrait of the Artist as a Young Man, *describes the epiphany before an object as a moment in which* "its soul, its whatness, leap to us from the vestment of its appearance. The soul of the commonest object ... seems to us radiant." It seems to me that it's impossible to think of a radiant, soulful object as [what Heidegger calls] standing reserve, as something that exists only for me to make use of as I will. I can't clearcut an acre of forest in which I recognize its whatness, its radiance. Poetic epiphany, by helping reveal the whatness and radiance of things and people, may thus be helpful in redressing some of the ecological imbalances we're currently living with.

In concert with many of these poets, I believe that what we perceive when we perceive being is resonance: the resonance of individual things with others, and the resonance of the whole; and the resonance of the whole *in* individual things. And I agree with Domanski that it is an experience available to anyone. Also in concert with many of these poets I find that immediate awareness of this resonance is wordless; and thinking about it, remembering it, reflecting on it, involves sustained attention to abstract and concrete images — kinaesthetic, aural, tactile, emotional, visual, and olfactory gestalts. In other words, the exercise of ontological attention demands imagination; it demands thinking in images. To repeat: the imagination in Auden's sense does not make things up. It perceives *what is there* in ways that calculative reason cannot.

Like Auden and Gustafson, I can also distinguish two *sorts* of awareness in the making of poetry: a wordy one and a wordless one, and, indeed, the wordless one usually comes first. Both, it seems to me, involve images — but the wordy, 'secondary' process involves something else as well: awareness of syntax and semantics, of sentential logic, of the definitions, connotations, and etymologies of words. Image-thought is importantly and fundamentally involved in trying to match the tone-qualities of language — the pitch and rhythm of words, their emotional resonance, the cadence of phrases and stanzas — to ontological experience. But words, unlike musical tones, carry all that *non*-imagey baggage, too — the very stuff that makes language especially suited to calculative reasoning. The 'secondary' aspect of poetry, then, is for me and many others, a fraught and paradoxical activity — a bit like trying to get a locomotive to dance or an accountant's ledger to sing. (Why do we do it? Why not paint or make music instead? Ah, there's an interesting question. But another one that must be reserved for a separate occasion.)

Although many poets — both historical and contemporary, in English and in other languages, in literate and in oral societies — have testified to the essential wordlessness of lyric intuition, their sense of the difficulty of throwing words at that intuition and discerning what sticks, and how, and why, varies. For Auden, I believe, it was not especially difficult: he was, I think, more at home with language as a medium than many. Still, he does make the distinction. There are some writers who, I sense, focus almost entirely on what Auden calls Secondary Imagination: the linguistic skin of the poem.

(Though if words and wordplay alone constitute the actual *stuff* of the piece, 'skin' is hardly an apt metaphor.) Such writing does not make the impression on me that what I *call* 'poetry' does; and poets as diverse as Wallace Stevens and P.K. Page have drawn a similar distinction, reserving the word 'poetry' for the kind of writing that has that non-linguistic 'interior.'

The last point I'd like to take up before we turn to the question of how, why, or if any of this matters is Auden's claim that, in negotiating the relationship between a poem's linguistic skin and its wordless innards, the Secondary Imagination always aims for the beautiful. Here, I am of one mind with Dennis Lee: the most fitting expression, the one that *fits best,* will be an *enactive* one: one that manages to make the experience, or its trace, live again in the imagination of the reader. Will this enactive expression always rise to the unmessy ideal of Victorian symmetry and restraint? No. (Imagine Ginsburg's "Howl" cast as a crown of sonnets.) As Auden himself notes, some experiences of the Primary Imagination are of "panic dread" — it's hard to imagine how a *fitting* expression of such experience could be squeezed into a corset or required to keep its spats clean. 'Beauty' is indeed a word that we often reach for when awe has brought us to our knees, and it is in fact something that I strive for in a good deal of what I write. But if we use the word as we often do — to stretch to poems like Sylvia Plath's "Lady Lazarus" or Paul Celan's "Tenebrae" — we are gesturing not at pleasantness or tidiness, but at something with great power, the chilling impersonality that Auden points to when he says the sacred is "humourless," the thing that Rilke points to when he says "das Schöne ist nichts / als des Schrecklichen Anfang, den wir noch grade ertragen" [*beauty is nothing but the beginning of terror, which we're just able to bear*]. It is true that sometimes we use 'beautiful' to point to something so delicate it takes our breath away. But it takes our breath away, I'd like to suggest, because of our simultaneous awareness of the enormity on whose brink it stands. Delicacy *points* to that enormity: it is an ontological category, in a way in which the small and the flimsy are not.

To sum up: yes, many poets do think, at least in outline, according to the model Auden describes. This does not mean that everything you find *called* poetry is going to exhibit both depth of ontological awareness and masterly enactive expression. Some of what gets called poetry, indeed, some writing that wins poetry prizes, is exclusively verbal pyrotechnics, and it pointedly, often explicitly, eschews any pretensions to ontological resonance or insight — a 'poetry' for our times, perhaps. And some of what gets called poetry — usually by our doting parents, or our kind friends, or ourselves, in the first flush of excitement at having got something down on the page — has its genesis in an experience of being, but is not 'fitting.' It fails to enact the experience for any reader who wasn't actually there. These social facts about the proliferation of non-poetry are, however, no cause for concern. Hucksters are and have been a fact of life in every culture; and the presence among us of closet poets, Sunday poets, and beginning poets of all levels of commitment is in fact a cause for rejoicing. It testifies to the power of ontological experience, to its widespread existence, and its existence in the most unlikely places. It confirms Auden's and Domanski's view that even in highly secular cultures there is a hunger for such experience. And perhaps — since it suggests that nothing can kill poetry — it means that Auden's poetic epistemology is relevant for more than a handful of oddballs hanging out on the fringes of a social order constructed by calculative reason.

This returns us to our final question, which we might phrase concisely as: So what?

To consider the significance of Auden's poetic epistemology, I'd like to contrast it with another, which we might call the epistemology of control. This epistemology is actually the epistemology of Baconian science, and, as such, one might think it had long been superseded by relativity theory and quantum physics. However, as a collection of ideological commitments, methods, and principles, Baconian science is still very much with us. Those commitments, first articulated by Bacon and Descartes in the seventeenth century, were later worked deeply into the texture of Western European culture through connections with new technologies and the growth of capitalism during the French Enlightenment. Now, in social sciences like economics, applied sciences like medicine, and, indeed, in most English-speaking humanities departments, the epistemology of control still encapsulates the ideal of expert and therefore 'genuine' knowing. This is the case even though, in many respects, Baconian science is more what non-scientists think science is than what actual theoretical scientists — especially, for example, physicists — now do. (Was Bacon himself a Baconian? Clearly he did not have Descartes's interest in mathematics, nor an interest in formal systems of any sort. But equally clearly, he did believe that humans ought to exert control over nature. Did he envision this control as remorseless domination? Can his use of the rhetoric of inquisition and bondage, applied to nature conceived as a female being, be excused by his broader aims? There has been considerable debate about these issues.)

Here are what the two epistemologies — Bacon's and Auden's — look like set side by side:

WAYS OF KNOWING

AUDEN'S POETIC EPISTEMOLOGY	THE EPISTEMOLOGY OF BACONIAN SCIENCE
• Epistemic duty: *To praise being*	• Epistemic duty: *To judge ("This is true, that isn't")*
• Epistemic attitude: *Gratitude*	• Epistemic attitude: *Suspicion*
• Purpose of knowing: *None*	• Purpose of knowing: *Control*
• Epistemic organ: *The imagination*	• Epistemic organ: *The mind*
• Litmus of certainty: *Awe (Primary Imagination); Sense of proportion (Secondary Imagination)*	• Litmus of certainty: *Systematic argument (that is, deductive relationships to self-evident premises or inductive relationships to reliable observations)*
• Evidence this is a genuine paradigm: *Our love of poetry; some cultures' need of poetry*	• Evidence this is a genuine paradigm: *The 'success' of science; Big Technology*

There are many features of interest that this comparison throws into relief. One is the generosity of Auden's epistemology, compared to the Baconian paradigm — if these were people, there's no question which we'd want to invite to dinner. Because of the contrast between imaginative engagement and intellectual control, there are also provocative echoes of Blake's cosmology. Then there's the very interesting fact that the poetic paradigm, unlike the Baconian one, apparently treasures knowledge for its own sake: for the poet, knowing, like being, simply *is*. In this respect, the poetic paradigm more closely embodies the scholarly ideal of knowledge for knowledge's sake than does the paradigm that underlies so much of what actually goes on in contemporary Western universities.

How are we to judge which of these paradigms is more worthy? Or if neither is, or both are?

Note that this question is being asked from *within* the epistemology of control: poetry's epistemology is being asked to submit itself to Baconian-style judgement. If we looked at them from poetry's vantage point, we would have to scan for the presence of the sacred; and this exercise would reveal that the chart and my discussion of it — indeed, nearly everything I've said here — reflects allegiance to the Baconian way of knowing!

This fact — that in the kind of discussion pursued in literate philosophical essays in the West we lead with questions and presentations from within the perspective of epistemological control, perhaps not even noticing that that's what we're doing — shows that in the West this way of knowing is thought of as *the* way of knowing. Why do Western thinkers think this?

It's partly cultural habit. But how or why was the habit acquired in the first place? It has to do, I believe, with the notion of *criteria*, the role that reasoned argument plays in the West's idea of how to establish truth. Explicit interest in criteria of justification emerged first in the seventeenth century, in connection with the new, mathematized science; and it was then developed in the Enlightenment as, in part, a demand for publicly acceptable reasons — a monarch's whim or bad mood was no longer an adequate ground for depriving someone of life, liberty, or personal property. At its root, then, in part, was the political ideal of equality of persons. In science, the demand for criteria became the defence against superstition (as we see, for example, in Diderot's *Encyclopédie,* as well as in Bacon's *Novum Organum*); and, ultimately, the demand for criteria is the reason that, as Auden says, contemporary Western culture does not countenance a robust distinction between the sacred and the profane: the sacred has been lumped together with superstition and dismissed.

Why has it been conflated with superstition? — Because, as Auden notes, the Primary Imagination is basically inarticulate: it perceives and knows but, unlike the Secondary Imagination, it cannot *argue* its point. It is therefore difficult to detect cases where someone is shamming. If *you* don't see a sacred being but someone else says she does, how are you to know whether or not to believe her? Baconian science claims to be able to give you a checklist.

But note that once again we've slipped into the Baconian way of thinking. It is true that the Primary Imagination cannot argue its case *in the Baconian style* — it does not respond well to prosecution. But what are profound poems and paintings, plays and musical compositions if not ways of trying to position an audience so that it, too, can perceive a sacred being?

If we reflect for a moment, we see that a similar challenge can be put to the methods of Baconian science itself. If a chemist says it's okay to drink DDT straight, or a civil engineer says the bridge is safe, or a logician claims that second order predicate calculus is incomplete, how do you know whether or not to believe her? If you're not especially good at inductive or deductive reasoning, even if you have all the data, what is obvious to the adept scientist or logician will not be at all obvious to you. Just as some people are better logicians or engineers than others, so some have better Primary Imaginations — they can perceive ontological resonance more quickly, more accurately, and in greater detail. But in all cases — logic, engineering, poetry, the other arts — any of us can learn to make the most of what we've got. We can exercise and discipline, sensitize and strengthen the capacities we have. Indeed, this was the essential vision of the humanities: that the study of art, literature, and music built depth and discernment of imagination just as the study of STEM subjects — science, technology, engineering, and mathematics — builds the discriminatory capacities of the deductive-inductive intellect.

Ultimately, an epistemology is a way of holding the world up to the light. If one way of holding it up reveals facets invisible to another, this tells us only that the world is complex. It does not tell us that one way is correct or better than the others; nor does it tell us that any way, at any given moment, for any given individual will do. It tells us that we need to be curious, and that we need to have patience and good will to sustain the curiosity; it tells us that we need to have courage in the face of the unfamiliar. In offering a genuine alternative to the Baconian paradigm, Auden's gesture is thus, at root, moral. In its specific content, it also speaks directly to one of the West's deepest cultural impoverishments: it reminds us that at times it is appropriate to relinquish control in favour of awe and praise. The refusal of this truth lies at the root of the ecological cataclysm we now face.

Wilderness and Agriculture

When the Wildlife Control Officer from the county came, he confirmed that we had a problem. "They'll take every tree within 200 yards either side." He was eager to set the dynamite and watch the dams go up but, having grown up hunting north of the Sault, he didn't like the part of his job that required him to kill beavers: "Don't shoot what you can't eat." But there was no point blowing the dams, he said, if you didn't kill the beavers, too — they'd just rebuild, usually overnight. He told me, trying to reassure me I think, that they weren't particularly "nice" critters: he'd seen them use traps, with the bodies of their dead kin still inside, to repair dynamited dams. Thinking about it later that evening I couldn't decide if this made them sinners, or saints.

~

There was no question I could get the county to do the work. Our fords had been destroyed, the banks were being seriously destabilized, we were losing fences and, arguably, the whole horse pasture might eventually be cut off — all of which meant your tax dollars could be spent on our farm to control beavers in the name of 'conservation.' And while it was nice to be invited to think of myself as a responsible eco-citizen making hard choices for the greater environmental good, it was pretty clear that accepting that invitation was just a way of simplifying and obscuring the real issues.

In the first place, there was my hopeless prejudice in favour of the trees: trees are profoundly beautiful. Think of what they do with light and wind, think of their patience, their vulnerability. And these particular trees — mostly poplars — their slimness and whiteness, the exquisite lisp of the aspens, the perfume of the balsams in late spring. Their presence along the riverbank, and the colonies in the east pasture and on Baldy (the oxymoronically named hummock in our south field) defined the visual presence of the farm. They constituted its margins which, as Wendell Berry has observed, are not only ecologically important, but essential to a certain sort of rhythmic pleasure humans take in landscape. (This is not to say that landscape without obvious margins can't give us aesthetic pleasure, simply that it gives us pleasure of a different, or sometimes more subtle, sort.) Anyway, no question that without the trees our farm would not be as easy on the eye. Nor would it look 'the way it had always looked' — that is, exist visually as a symbol of historical permanence, of my present's continuity with my past.

So: very convenient for me that the course of 'conservation' turned out to be the path of least resistance. I could tell I wanted to be beguiled — but precisely because I could tell that, it wasn't happening. So what was wrong with wanting to save trees? Why was the coincidence of private desire and public policy making me uneasy?

Once I'd put the question in those terms, the answer seemed pretty obvious: both were serving the interests of a certain way of appreciating nature, a way that was arguably opposed to the interests of nature itself. Or to put it another way: the trees stood at the interface between wilderness and agriculture — me on one side, the beavers on the other — and my unease stemmed neither from private scruple nor ecological complexity, but simply from the fraught, puzzling nature of that interface itself. Western Europeans and their postcolonial descendants have, in the last hundred years, discovered that it won't work to proceed as if agriculture had no relation to wilderness; but they still have very little idea what an ecologically healthy version of that relation might look like.

One of my friends once remarked, as though it constituted a *reductio ad absurdum* of environmentalists' views, "Why, they're even against *agriculture!*" Er, but when you stop to think about it, what's so crazy about that? The suggestion that humans require agriculture — or at least the current North American version of it — to survive as a species is patently false; while the suggestion that it has been responsible for massive environmental damage both on this continent and elsewhere is indisputably true. "Well," my skeptical friend might continue, "that's not a problem with agriculture *itself*, it's a problem with the way it's practised, with its scale." This, though, begs the key question: it assumes there's some other scale, acceptable to most contemporary North Americans, on which agriculture might be practised. But European, colonial, and postcolonial agriculture are not phenomena independent of patterns of settlement and exchange, economies and trade, population densities and, nowadays, corporate profit. To change the style and scale of agriculture would be to change Euro-colonial culture *as a whole*. What my friend wants is what we've got, with maybe the odd design modification. What environmentalists have seen is that that desire is not sustainable in the long run. In a way, my friend is right: it is the scale, not the fact, of some human culturing relation to land that's the problem. But to change the scale significantly would be to change everything else about the way we live.

~

What is wilderness? Typically, we think of it as 'unsullied' nature, nature in its 'natural' state. But push on this a little and two further assumptions emerge: that there are (or have been) portions of the earth completely unaffected by human activity; and that human activity is, by definition, unnatural. I'm not so sure about either of these claims. I agree that a great deal of what my own culture does and advocates in relation to nonhumans is wrong, unhealthy, and disruptive of relatively stable cycles of growth and decline. I agree that its practices themselves fail to exhibit the complexity, rhythm, and balance that are hallmarks of many natural processes. But none of this has to do with what is essentially *human*: it has to do with a particular ideological inheritance.

And, although we are now, globally, confronting what Bill McKibben in the late '80s called "the end of nature," I don't see how the ecological truths underlying the demise weren't ever thus. What members of my culture are at last coming to realize is that the planet constitutes an astonishingly complex whole, composed of many disparate but interacting sub-systems, themselves made up of smaller sub-systems. But this fact has not been *created* by environmental crisis; it is something that environmental crisis merely makes more visible. As long as there have been humans on the earth, their activities, like those of all other beings, have in more and less subtle ways affected the smaller and larger ecologies in which they have occurred. Because PCBs, micro-plastics, nitrogen in chemical fertilizers, lead from car exhaust, mercury from the industrial production of chlorine, to say nothing of carbon dioxide and methane, are harmful above certain concentrations, and especially because my culture has produced a lot of them, we are now *aware* of human presence where we were not aware of it before. But the atmosphere and oceans have always dispersed, carried, and concentrated various human by-products. If human activity is unnatural, and therefore defiling of the wild, there hasn't been any true wilderness for at least 200,000 years.

"Wait a minute," someone might say, "you're missing the point. Nobody's going to deny that humans have always been mixed up in their environment. But there's something different in kind about the abominations introduced by late twentieth-century Euro-American warfare and industrial capitalism. Of course 'wilderness' doesn't mean 'no campfires'; but it does mean 'no strontium 90.'" Does it, though? Is it the bare presence or absence of certain substances — however minuscule their quantities, and however produced — that determines the presence or absence of wilderness? (Suppose lightning, striking some dust gathered for ceremonial purposes, produces a molecule or two of strontium 90....) Well, no: quantity is a factor — and, it would appear, so is motive.

These observations, taken together with the inevitability of ecological interaction between humans and their environments, are why I want to argue that wilderness depends not on the absence of human interaction with the land, but rather on its quantity and style. Wilderness exists, I want to suggest, to a greater or lesser degree, wherever we allow communities of nonhumans to shape us at least as much as or more than we shape them. (If you think no such openness presently occurs anywhere, and has no possibility of occurring in the future, you'll want to cast that last sentence irrevocably in the past tense.)

Trevor Herriot, in his searching and perceptive chronicle of the Qu'Appelle, comes at the issue from the other side:

> Most of our problems began when we hammered our hunting spears into ploughshares. From that point on, it has been one valley after another — Euphrates, Nile, Ganges, Rhine, Seine, St Lawrence, Mississippi, Hudson — eviction of the local hunter-gatherers and pastoralists, replacing them with farmers who soon multiply, filling the valley with a civilization that venerates the tiller's short-term residency, calling this 'settlement,' while dismissing the hunter's long-term residency, several thousand years of seasonal migration and ecological congruency as mere 'nomadism.'

It is not, in other words, human culturing that destroys wilderness; it is the manner of that culturing and the attitude behind it. Many human societies have negotiated the border with the non-human world in a way that has permitted both sides to flourish. In places, fragments of some societies continue to do so, and in other places, fragments of other societies are trying to learn how — thinning and weeding, aerating and fertilizing, burning and irrigating, all with the aim of increasing the health and complexity of various plant communities and thereby their own harvest. What genuinely sustainable human cultures have *not* done is break thousands of acres of sod, or clear-cut even one acre of forest, or fish with dragnets; they have not aimed to eliminate whole communities of native species in order to promote dependence on non-native cultivars. Above all, their populations have stayed relatively low in relation to the populations of the wild species they have lived, or live, among.

Viewed from this perspective, *wilderness* and *agriculture* are not dichotomously opposed terms that, between them, exhaust the possibilities. Rather, it begins to look as though agriculture is a term that mediates between the nonhuman and its exploitation — a.k.a. industrial logging, corporate fisheries or, more generally, agribiz. The Greek word we usually translate as 'wild' is *agrios,* which means literally 'of the field'; but it is formed from the word *agros,* field, which is the root of the word *agriculture.* In this etymology the wild and the cultivated come from the same place, the field that accommodates and sustains them both. Agribiz, by contrast, sees the field only as the arena of short-term capital profit. In such a field, there is no room for wilderness, nor, for that matter, culture in its broader sense.

But what does this mean for our farm? Surely we're not engaged in agribiz? We've got less than half a section under cultivation, low till, no pesticides, herbicides, or chemical fertilizers, we use small equipment. ... Yes, but there wouldn't be a beaver 'problem' on sw32-57-08-w5, if the land those numbers designated weren't 'in production,' if the poplars and spruce and willow hadn't been cleared from everything except the banks, hummocks, and steep hillsides. The beavers could take as much as they wanted, and the course of the river wouldn't be destabilized if the place were still wild. There'd still be plenty of balsam and aspen left for the occasional human, passing through, to enthuse over.

Is this, then, the direction of a solution: to campaign for a reduction in human population, a return to a less exploitative way of life, and in the meantime to put the farm back down to trees and leave the beavers be? Perhaps. But even this proposal — maybe I'm just kidding myself? — seems to bear the stamp of insufficient subtlety and complexity. It forgets that individuals, like cultures, are ecologies of history and desire. While my planetary-thinking head recognizes the ecological wisdom of the suggestion, my locally-acting heart isn't sure it's up to it. My grandparents *homesteaded* this place. My mother, when I put it to her, couldn't imagine it. And it wasn't only because of the change in the landscape. It was also because of all that labour, the struggle that it represented, the hopes that fed it, the violence it required — there is indeed something shocking, in a deep physical sense, about thinking it might all have been a mistake. More difficult, I find, than wondering if the human species itself might be an evolutionary dead-end. It's more like trying to think through whether you yourself should have been born.

And here's something else. I can't think of a non-agribizcious society that, as a female, I'd be willing to choose over the one I already belong to. This could easily be because I haven't read enough, or it could be because what I've read has been filtered through English-speaking patriarchy. I know there's a wing of feminist analysis that locates women's oppression in the advent of private property, which itself seems to have begun with ownership of herd animals. But if what I've read about the sexual division of labour in many pre-colonial cultures is correct, or about the political privileges of women even in societies that trace descent matrilineally, I'm not at all sure that reversion to such a way of life — even if it were possible — represents an ideal I could aspire to. There's a link between the Enlightenment's attempt to use science to better the human lot and the rate at which, as a culture, the West has exploited the wild. There's also a link between that vision and the political emancipation of women — including their ability to choose whether or not they're going to bear children.

What, then, should I do? How to balance personal loyalty, ecological common sense, political realism, aesthetic inclination, and cultural guilt, and leave room for the play of all those things I know I don't know enough about, and possibilities I can't yet imagine? I don't know. If wilderness is not chaos but complex living pattern, it can, at least to some extent, be understood. But if it is complex living pattern and not a dissociated array of raw materials, then that understanding will consist of more than a set of facts about the bottom line. Coming to it would be a bit like learning how to dance. It would require musicality, patience, social courage, attention to the other, and, above all, time.

We might even say that the acquisition of such virtues — the co-ordinated wisdom of *agros* and *agrios* that members of Western European colonial cultures might have allowed the nonhuman to teach us — is what culture is about. But time is not a virtue. Time, as Anaximander suggested several centuries ago, is the judge of virtue, that which assesses the justice or injustice of all coming-to-be and passing-away. Time is what neither I nor the poplars, neither the farm nor the beavers, have anymore. In its absence, we must choose without discernment, and any principled action we might take will carry the taint of imposed, rather than responsive, order. In its absence we will fail to enact an agricultural relation even to the wildernesses of our own lives.

Once upon a Time in the West: Heidegger and the Poets

Well, I'll tell ya — I been hearin a lot about that Marty Heidegger lately. Ain't been in for a while, but he used to show up pretty regular. Didn't care much for his politics, but he was the best shot with a Mannlicher-Schonauer I ever seed. What I been hearin is mostly from poets — well, an folks as read poetry, too — mostly 'bout that Primal Speech therapy he was gettin them into. Now I sure agree the world'd be a better place if we all thought it *should* be run by writers, instead of *bein* run by transnationals. My problem's with what thinkin of yerself as a poet the way Heidegger means it does to your ability to pay attention to things, to really listen to an look at the world, see'r for how she is instead of what you want 'er to be. We all like to think we're doin our bit for the search posse, an Marty's given the poets' egos a boost there; but if you really get what he's gettin at, it's not quite so simple as thinkin poets come up with a kinder gentler way of runnin camp. An to really get what he's gettin at you gotta go back years — hell, you could go back to before these parts was ever opened up if you wanted the whole story. But you ain't got all night, have ya, so I'll try to keep it short an start with what happened when Manny Kant got wind of that strike over on Dave Hume's place.

See, Manny was smarter'n most folks. He got to thinkin about it an he realized that if Dave had found what he said he found, then all of science — leastways, science as we like to think about it, laws'n stuff — was in trouble. If Hume'd got it right, then science couldn't be certain — that was the problem. Why, maybe you take this whiskey bottle here, an this time when you hold 'er out'n let 'er go, instead of fallin, she flies off out the window, or up over your head. You can't *prove* to yerself before you do it what she's gonna do. Yeah — you think all them Laws of Science, they prove it. But that's just the point: how you gonna know they're *laws* an not just what science types call *statistical generalizations* — sorta summaries of the fact that a heap of things *happen* to've happened the same way? Dave Hume says that's 'zactly what they are, an it's only outta *habit* you think she's gonna fall on the floor instead of doin somethin else.

But Manny, he's thinkin, "Uh oh — what if science ain't certain?" an it hits him: "Wait a minute — if it's just a habit I think the bottle's gonna fall, well then that habit can be broken." So he tries to seriously think the bottle's gonna do somethin different — imagines himself holdin it out there, squeezin his eyes right up he's tryin so hard — but: he can't do it! An, he says, neither can you. Go ahead'n try — you get serious with yerself about this, you can't do it no matter what. Well, then, it can't be no habit, can it? Still, that ol' Hume: he was right it ain't like a truth of logic or a definition — you gotta have some experience of the world before it'll hit you. You gotta get out there an fool around with whiskey bottles some. So how come you can know it, for *certain,* but it ain't a truth of logic? Well, this was Kant's real red ribbon idea: he says it's like there's these filters in your head, like you got some sorta hard-wired circuitry. Everythin from the outside's gotta come through the filters before it gets to the inside — but the inside's where *you* is. So everythin you see, it's been sorta sorted — pre-shaped, like — before it gets to you. You can tell them filters're in there cuz of you bein *certain* that everythin you see is gonna be in 3-D *an* it's gonna obey the Laws of Science. Now them Laws of Science — they ain't *laws* exactly, "Thou shalt not" 'n all. They're more like names for ways stuff tends to hang together. So Causality, fr'instance — that's the sorta thing Manny Kant'd call a Law of Science: some stuff *causes* other stuff, it ain't just whacks of totally similar coincidences. An that's why you don't stop to ask yerself every time you're fixin to haul off'n throw your coffee cup at the wall, "Now, this time, is it gonna head in the direction I throw it? Oh dear, is it gonna hit the wall'n make a mess?" Course it is, an Manny says you know it. Not cuz the Laws of Science're like Decrees of God'r somethin; we don't know nothin about God at this point. Nope, them Laws of Science, they're like the diagram for the hard-wirin; an they ain't 'out there,' in the world, cuz that circuitry's 'in here,' in your head. But they sure are certain. Ain't nothin gonna register in that ol' noggin of yers but what it's been filtered'n set up by that hard-wirin. So *that's* why you can't break the habit of thinkin the whiskey bottle's gonna drop: you're hard-wired to see the world in causal 3-D, an lettin 'er go *causes* 'er to fall.

Then Hegel comes along. Now, ol' George was one long-winded sonnuva side-show host — history, he thought you had to do all of history over agin before you could say "How de do" — but he finally gets his checkers lined up an he says to Kant, "Well y'know, Manny, this hard-wirin idea of yers, it's pretty good. I like it. Gonna get me one too. But — where d'ya think the circuitry diagram comes from? You start with that thing from Descartes, 'I think therefore I am,' you say the 'I am' bit is just totally obvious, an you build your case from there. But, hell, Manny, you just *stole* the circuitry diagram from Aristotle without thinkin where he got it from or if it was even what you actually needed, an if we're *really* hard-wired then the 'I am' bit's also gotta be obvious *because* of the hard-wirin, not as somethin separate that twigs you to the fact the hard-wirin's there, if you see what I mean. Hmmm. Well, maybe you don't. I admit it's kinda tricky. What I mean is: you say there's stuff Out There'n it comes 'in' through the filters'n gets shaped by the circuitry. But listen, Manny — how can we actually *know* that? You say the unfiltered stuff comin through the filters *causes* us to have experience of filtered stuff — no input, no output, right? But ain't Cause one of the filters? So even sayin that, you're thinkin filtered. No way we can ever have any idea Whatsoever of Anythin that ain't been filtered. But if it's been filtered, it's 'in here' not Out There.

"So," George says to Manny, "so, No. 1, there can't really be no 'in here' 'n 'out there,' it's *all* gotta be the same thing, an that thing is Thought, an No. 2, if you think hard about why you went ahead 'n just reached for yr Aristotle or why Aristotle come up with the categories you borrowed for yr diagram, you'll realize it's all in the *language* you speak — whatever that happens to be. So Thought is the only stuff there is, an, even more important — *this* is the totally important thing, Manny — Thought itself is made of Language. It's made of Language."

Now I wanna rein in a minute so's we can see where we've got to. We starts with this worry about the nature of scientific laws — gotta figure out why we just can't change our minds about 'em — an we end up here: language is all there is. Now, c'mon. You can git your head awhirlin, all these fancy-dress ideas dancin an spoonin an you-know-what-else with each other, but if the place it gets you is there ain't no chairs'n tables, ain't no paper you're readin this on, ain't no TMX or bees or C-O-two, ain't *nothin* 'out there' *but what we didn't say it first,* cuz there ain't no 'out there' to begin with, an what Is's only what our pappies 'n our granpappies *said* — for all of History 'n creation — well, I say "Whoa, Nellie!" I say you're willin to go along with that, you ain't never gone more'n half'n hour with an empty belly, you ain't never seen nobody have a heart attack in fronta you or been caught out on the prairie in a thunderstorm. Now I'm not sayin our minds don't sometimes bend things outta shape, an I'm not sayin some of 'em don't look different if you come from Lapland 'stead of New Jersey, but I *am* sayin if you let either multiculturalism 'r modern metaphysics convince ya *you* (or you-'n-yr-gang) are the Author of the World, you stopped payin attention to the bran in your Wheaties some time ago.

Which brings us to this fella Marty Heidegger. (Sorry, we're kinda skippin over some of th'other guys who've called in at this saloon in between — but Fred Nietzsche, Ed Husserl, an them other boys, they're mostly just yellin "Set 'em up, George.") Anyways, this Heidegger fella, he comes in, has a drink or two — George is still pourin — shoots the shit a while, an then he says, "Fellas, time we called this dickin around quits. This crap about who's with what gang, do Ed's boys grind their coffee finer than Fred's, it's all a dead end. Time we talked about somethin that matters around here. Time we had ourselves a poetry readin." An he stands up on that table over there an starts chantin this stuff about gods 'n savin powers 'n the Light of Bein. Well, you can imagine. An the poets, a few who mostly'd just dropped in for a quick drink, they're goin crazy, whoopin'n hollerin through the door for all the others t'come on in.

But the thing you gotta remember about Marty is, first, he went to Jesuit school before he got his spurs, an, more important, even though he don't usually say too much about it, him'n George, they go a long way back. An I mean a *long* way back. So even though he's talkin about the world an the gods an stars an mountains, what he's really thinkin is: it's all language, all language, flat as a pancake, fur as the eye can see. What he means when he says, "Man is not the lord of bein's, he's the Shepherd of Bein" ain't quite "Quit drivin a loggin truck an go join the Sisters of Charity." Yeah, I mean, that's kinda a part of what he's meanin cuz of the Jesuit thing'n all, but the big part, the *main* part is: it's not that there's Things an they're Out There an you gotta take care of 'em; unh-uh; it's that human language equals Thought equals the Whole Sheebang. It's all happenin in here (except there ain't no 'in here' cuz there ain't no Out There), inside (except there ain't no 'inside' cuz there ain't no 'outside') the li'l ol' noggin. You're not makin it up exactly, cuz Language — the hard-wirin — it's imposin what your analytic types'd call constraints. But in another sense y'are makin it up — cuz there ain't nothin exists separate of your knowin it. If it weren't for us Language-speakers, wouldn't be no Bein to corral.

Now, says Marty, better you should be a poet with all this goin on than a technocrat. An I agree with you that part sounds pretty good. But you gotta ask why he says it. Turns out he says it cuz he thinks technocrats *forgit* it's all Language. They think there's stuff, separate from them, really Out There. An that, of course, is their Big Mistake. Yeah, they shouldn't do the calculatin, utilizin, Rhine-Valley-Hydroelectric-Project thing — but they only do it cuz they don't realize the world ain't really out there; all that calculatin, utilizin stuff, it's just a *symptom* of the deeper problem. See, for Marty, the Jesuit-school boy, the Whole Sheebang's 'destinin,' by which he means followin its appointed course, by which he means whatever's happenin, however bad it might look to us, hasta, in some way, be a version of what the Whole Sheebang *wants* to do. An he's got this really complicated argument — part Greek, part Hegel, part fancy-pants German etymology — that what it *wants* to do is go'n hide. What better way to hide than get dressed up as your exact opposite — a.k.a. the appearance that the world is Really Out There — an go hang out with the bad guys who're pushin that idea to extinction? If we really wanna unmask Big Science an show Bein for what she is, then we don't stop the technocrats calculatin, we show 'em that their calculatin is a *way* of constitutin Bein, a *way* of bein an Author of the World. An, of course, as soon as they see *that,* they're gonna wanna write a different book, a *poetry* book — all about Us, the Language-Possessors, the Greek-temple-with-a-view-of-the-sea Architects an Developers of that world class property, the House of Bein.

So my first itch about the Heidegger'n Poets jamboree is those guys ain't noticed who's payin the rent on the hall: Marty didn't come up with mosta this stuff himself, he found it out in George's shed, an George'd borrowed it from Manny, who built it in the first place cuz he was afraid of Dave Hume. Now it's true Marty's put his own decorations up, an foregroundin the 'appointed course' stuff as 'destinin' rather than Dialectic is a part of that. But it's just plain wrong to think the whole business is some bran new homestead broke with the poets in mind or that Marty filed his claim on it cuz he didn't like machines. Yeah, sure, technology bugged him — but it ain't where the ideas come from, an it ain't where they're goin neither.

But shit, we all do that sometimes, forgit where stuff comes from. I ain't told ya much about Kant owin Gotty Leibnitz or Hume'n Nick of Autrecourt, have I? An I ain't hardly mentioned René Without Whom or all the stuff Heidegger got from them medieval dudes. So maybe I'm too suspicious of hype an probably as guilty as anybody else of presentin things outta context. What I really want t'get you thinkin about is this Role of the Poet stuff, language as the House of Bein, an poetry as Primal Speech. What Marty's stuff means is partly where it comes from — an tryin to get at that's been mostly the point of the history lesson. Like I say, when Marty tells you "Bein's poem, just begun, is man," that ain't no metaphor. He means without us, without human language, there ain't nothin — not even Nothin.

Yeah, yeah, you say, but sayin thought is bein an language is thought, that don't mean the mushrooms an the railway tracks are *make believe.* You say they're real, alright, they're as real as it gets. It's just that their reality is, well, like the reality of everythin else — it *comes from* bein Thought. An of course it's us as is doing the Thinkin even while we're bein Thought (by Thought) ourselves. But I say all that just sounds like some kinda politics to me — either the kind where it don't matter what anyone does or says cuz the Thinkin's just gonna roll on over 'em whether they keep runnin or not, or the kind where the Pawnee depends on us whities to Realize his or her True Potential. You think we really pay attention to the world or the things in it either way? I'm not sayin you *can't* think of the world like that. I know there's no way I can prove with some argument that that's not the way she is; an yeah, I even know that if I try, whatever argument I come up with's gonna Always Already be set on self-deconstruct. But seems to me that's a problem with arguments, not a problem with the world.

I know: you're gonna say the logic's so damn obvious it's crazy to pretend there's any real alternative. We can't know nothin about stuff we don't know nothin about; an if we *know* it, it's a knowee. But there's no knowee without a knower an no knower without his'r her perspective, a.k.a. axe to grind, whether that axe's communal property with a Destiny'r whether it's a hackin an a hewin at random. Language just *is* the way the mind carves the world up. An the only world we got is the world as we know it. So thinkin the world exists without human language, you're gonna say, is like thinkin one side of a coin exists without t'other side. OK. But it's also so damn obvious the world *is* out there, an that we *don't* bring it into bein. So in the end we gotta choose: between the obviousness of what logic tells us an the obviousness of the world bein out there. It's not a choice most folks is real happy about makin once they get to thinkin about it. An of course even if you don't leap for logic, you gotta admit the world depends on us *now* cuz we're set to finish 'er off — well, this version of 'er anyways, some of them fungi'll probably make it whatever we do. Question is whether you really believe once the seaweed 'n the clubmoss 'n the hydrological cycle's gone, some session of Speakin the Holy in an underground mall's gonna bring 'er back.

That's what I think poets're missin about Marty. Technocracy's just a symptom allright. The disease is thinkin human language creates the world. An I don't just mean the ol' Protestant pot-bangin against pride, though I probably mean that too. I mean somethin about *how* we pay attention to things. An I think we pay attention to 'em different if we think we're doin 'em a favour (like missionaries for the natives) than if we think they're out there on their own, doin just fine thank you, irregardless of us. Y'know the kinda guy who's so nice to his li'l lady — buyin 'er clothes, sendin 'er to them cookin classes, payin for the hairdresser — an then she up'n leaves 'im anyways? Well, why's that happen, d'ya spose? He was payin lots've attention to 'er. But turns out it weren't the right kind — he was payin attention to 'er as a way of payin attention to himself, he weren't actually payin attention to *her*. *Even* if you're a poet an not a nasty White imperialistic techno-patriarchal sonnuva bitch, if you think you're special cuz you make Bein happen, you're still gonna be attendin to stuff like it's your party, not like maybe it ain't nobody's party. Like maybe there ain't no party at all. Yeah, Marty useta get drunk with the farmers sometimes — but that's cuz they were Volk an spoke German. I know I said George said Thought's made of whatever language you speak, but I was sorta tryin to give him the benefit of the doubt. George actually thought Thought was pretty much Greek an German. He thought it was sorta alive too, an growin, an whatever it looked like now was cuz of what had happened in Greece 'n Germany in the old days. So it's not only that Bein's identical with human Thought an human Thought's identical with Language (specially some versions of it) — the Whole Sheebang's evolvin in the course of History, a.k.a. the Romantic version of the story of European art'n ideas. Marty didn't ask no questions about any of that. Nineteenth-century German long-hairs talked about farmers knowin the "dampness an richness of the soil," "the loneliness of the field-path as the evenin falls," "the silent call of the earth, its quiet gift of the ripenin grain," "uncomplainin anxiety as to the certainty of bread," "the wordless joy of havin once more withstood want." Ever notice how it never rains for two weeks on end? An how they *don't* talk about backaches an beatin your wife an malnutrition an class hatred? —So anyways, farmers bein these cool dudes, it was okay to drink with 'em. It's not cuz Marty knew farmin for what it was an wasn't a snob. It's just another case of him thinkin the brand makes the cow.

Now some folks is gonna say, "Whyn't we just take the idea of the poet as someone real precious, as the Shepherd of Bein, like, without all t'other fuss 'n feathers? Poets get a bad enough rap in these parts, Shelley notwithstandin," they'll say, "they've had it with unacknowledgement. They've been pinin for a philosophical lookin ever since Plato took it away from 'em. Why not say 'Language is the House of Bein' an mean Bein is delicate 'n sensitive 'n needs protectin; an poets, who're sposed to be good with words, can help out in this important task without any puffed up ideas that they're doin any more than holdin the door open'r makin sure the plumbin's fixed. They can *care* about Bein — an Marty's gang'll make sure they get fed while they're doin it — without thinkin they're makin it happen." —Well, I spose you could say somethin like that, but point is, then you're sorta cheatin: the size of the bore on Marty's ideas about pattin poets on the back comes from them bein part of a whole philosophy, a philosophy of a big time philosopher. It's a bit like buyin a car cuz it's painted green an made by a company with a big rep an not checkin to see if what's under the hood actually meets emission control standards. Other thing is, if you just buy the dessert without the main course, you're sorta treatin Marty the way some guys treat gals: you're not lookin at the thing as she is, you're lookin at 'er for what you want 'er to be.

Don't get me wrong. It'd be dumb to think there ain't some big questions here. Like I say, whatever you decide to hang on to come hell'r high water, downstream's a weird 'n scary place. If you think it's obvious the world is out there, turns out you hafta give up on bein able to provide a proof for how you know that. If you think it's obvious you gotta be able to provide a proof of how you know stuff or you can't really call it Knowin — could be just Believin (which we know it ain't) or worse, what Dave called Habit — you end up havin' to say it's all happenin inside your head. Or, as George'd say, that there ain't no 'outside' of the 'inside' of your head: your head just is The World. Real problems either way. An no wigglin away from the fact that in the end the choice ain't logical, it ain't even epistemological. It's moral.

Yep, in the end no amount of arguin'r analyzin's gonna tell ya which way to jump. Believin it will's just another way of sayin you already bought your ticket for the Modern European Philosophy stagecoach. The logic choppin's only gonna get you to the point where you can see you gotta choose on some other grounds. I said them grounds was moral cuz basically you're decidin what sorta person you wanna be, how you wanna see your responsibilities — an decidin to ride with Marty's boys or not is just one more way of answerin the question. You're pickin the set of problems you'd rather live with: bein the front page story, or not bein able to connect some kinds of knowin with logic. Seems to me thinkin we're the front page story ain't got such a hot track record. Not that you can't think you're the front page story *an* think logic don't always get you where you wanna go — guess that'd be one way of describin fascism. But to give yerself no gate in the fence, to say Bein *needs* human language or it ain't gonna survive: fascism'r no, I don't think that's gonna make for very good poets in the end. The love story of us 'n our reflection — not real catchy, is it. As for human language — no, you're right I can't prove it, but as fur as I can tell she ain't no House, she ain't even a lean-to: she's just a crusta caked mud stops us from seein what's unnerneath. Dust in the wind. Relyin on poets to use it to get us to the promised land's a bit like waitin for Nero's next fiddle tune to go platinum so's your toga won't get singed. That's why anybody, even Marty Heidegger, tells me poets is more important in the scheme of things than small-eyed horny toads or cut-leaf sage, I'm gonna ask 'em how the last chapter goes — it's comin up pretty fast — before I buy the book.

Lyric Realism: Nature Poetry, Silence, and Ontology

What is a nature poet? Until recently, the phrase often conjured a writer of sentimental quatrains about birds and sunsets, happy (or melancholic) rambles o'er hill and dale. As environmental concerns have come to dominate headlines, though, the term has taken on a less mawkish colouring: nature, it turns out, is a matter of serious, indeed urgent, interest. And it is clear, if we read Edward Thomas, say, or Mary Oliver, or Randy Lundy, that we should resist the amateurish stereotype: it is possible to be both brilliant and original and to take the natural world as one's subject. (As these examples indicate, it is also possible to be a nature poet and write about other things as well.) However, I want to suggest that a definition that focuses exclusively on content will also miss the point: the nature poet is not *simply* someone whose subject matter lies out of doors. The nature poet is, first and foremost, someone who does not doubt the world is real — or, more precisely, someone who would resist the suggestion that the world is a human construct, a thing that depends on human speaking or knowing to exist.

Well, who wouldn't? you might say. But in the Western tradition, many who most concern themselves with literature and the humanities are persuaded by the thought, common since the seventeenth century, that mind-independent realities do not exist. It is one of the reasons nature poetry, so called, remains a marginalized genre; and it is at the core of its political importance. The fundamental gestures that underlie nature poetry as I am defining it insist not that nature is nice but that it's *out there*: other than us, and every bit as ontologically robust. The nature poet is, indeed, frequently attracted to those bits of the world that we think of as 'natural': forests and rivers, mountains, foxes, prairies, swallows and frogs. But what I'm suggesting is that the particular subject matter, while frequently an indicator, should not be regarded as the essence. The essence is a commitment to acknowledging, mourning, and celebrating *what-is* — its non-, its extra-, and its fully human dimensions. This essence aligns the contemporary nature poet not only with the old ontologists of the European Presokratic tradition — Demokritos, Empedokles, Herakleitos — but with the Presokratics' near-contemporary of the Zhōu Dynasty, the author of the *Dào Dé Jīng*. Indeed, as what Western philosophers would call a 'realist,' the nature poet is closer to the non-writing thinkers of a number of Indigenous traditions than to anyone, critic or creative writer, for whom the business of language has replaced the world.

~

Konrad Lorenz, in *Behind the Mirror,* remarks:

> Any person not "sicklied o'er with the pale cast" of philosophical thought will regard it as utterly perverse to believe that the everyday objects around us become real only through our experience of them.... The notion that [the world] should become reality only when humans, here today and gone tomorrow, happen to notice it, strikes a person of nature, be they farmer or biologist, as not only preposterous but completely blasphemous.

That is, most people who have been led by choice or forced by occupation truly to pay attention to the nonhuman world will find the argument that its being is somehow derivative of human mental or linguistic capacities not merely unconvincing but *irreverent.* In saying this, Lorenz is not presupposing a commitment to any form of dogmatic religion. He is, rather, observing that reverence — care — is inextricably bound up with looking and listening. Really looking. Really listening.

David Abram, paraphrasing Maurice Merleau-Ponty, writes:

> ... other shapes and species have coevolved, like ourselves, with the rest of the shifting earth; their rhythms and forms are composed of layers upon layers of earlier rhythms, and

in engaging them our senses are led into an inexhaustible depth.... Whenever we assume the position and poise of the human animal... then the entire material world itself seems to come awake and speak.

I would like to rephrase this slightly. For the nature poet, it is not that when we pay close, animal-bright attention the world *seems* to come awake and to speak. When we pay attention, we can tell that the world *is* awake, that it means, hugely and richly, all the time. It is humans who — distracted, insecure, ill, battered by urban noise and electronic media — are not able to perceive what is in front of them.

~

That the natural world is an inexhaustible source of meaning, directly available to us if we allow our contemplative attention to rest there, is the theme of many poems by the Chinese recluse Xiè Língyùn. Xiè is the founding figure of the Rivers and Mountains tradition in Chinese poetry. He lived in the fifth century of the Common Era, in the politically chaotic period of the Six Dynasties. Here is an example of his work:

CLIMBING GREEN-CLIFF MOUNTAIN IN YǑNGJIĀ

> *Taking rice and a light staff,*
> *I walk with slow delight up to my secluded home.*
>
> *Along the stream, the path twists and grows distant,*
> *and as I take to the land, my heart continues to rejoice.*
>
> *The clear shallows are knotted in winter's shapes,*
> *the reflected bamboo glowing beneath the frost.*
>
> *A steep watercourse, and the rapids frothing away.*
> *Forests curve into the distance, and the cliffs crowd in.*

> *I gaze west and say it's the new moon,*
> *look back, and wonder if it's the setting sun.*
>
> *I tread the light of evening and rest in the dusky dawn,*
> *sheltered in a deep expanse of shadow.*
>
> *As the good book says, "Upper trigram* Venom: *value not serving.*
> *The perseverance of the recluse brings good fortune."*
>
> *One who lives in obscurity will always walk on the level,*
> *his goal as difficult as it is beautiful.*
>
> *Yes* this *and no* that — *what distinction?*
> *Silent, I embrace the One.*
>
> *And calm, as though already finished with everything articulate:*
> *healed nature is born from this.*

The undoing of the articulate by silence, the distinction between *yes this* and *no that* lost: there is indeed mystery here. How could such contemplation be thought appropriate for a poet? Poetry's *business* is words: if the result of attentive immersion in the unselfed, nonhuman world is the breakdown of linguistic thought, then this sort of absorption can't be the aim of the nature poet, under any definition. Can it?

Well, surprisingly enough, it seems the answer is 'yes.' There are echoes of Xiè Língyùn's sentiments in poets as diverse as William Wordsworth and Robert Hass, Jane Hirshfield and Tim Lilburn, Liz Philips and Gary Snyder. What are we to make of this? How does the nature poet understand the relation between human language and the nonhuman world?

Answering this question properly would take more space than I have here, so let me cut to the chase: nature poets are a species, a large species, of a genus we might call 'lyric thinkers.' By this term I do *not* mean Romantic self-aggrandizing expressers of personal emotion; in fact, I mean almost the opposite. A lyric thinker is someone whose understanding is driven by intuitions of coherence. Her experience, in this respect, can only be gestured towards, not captured, in a medium like language — whose use insists on distinctions of a type that are absent in lyric awareness. A nature poem, in this sense, is, then, never more than a finger pointing at the moon: its words do not 'contain' reality, but merely tell us in what direction we should look. Moreover, that this is all the nature poem is — a kind of ontological signpost — is a fact of which the person who has written it is usually acutely aware. Nature poetry's business is not actually words; it is the practice, the discipline, of coming home to the unselfed world.

Being human, and so being disposed to acquire and use language, the lyric thinker attempts to bring together words and the experience of ontological integrity. But this is a difficult task. With Freud I believe that neurophysiological conditions that must be present for language-use incidentally give rise to a phenomenological sense of self, a sense of being something distinct from one's environment. To be 'disposed to acquire and use language,' then, is to possess the potential for ontological alienation, a potential realized profoundly in gestures of exploitation, in viewing things as mere objects. (I should add that I don't believe this to be an exclusively human predicament.) There is considerable evidence that the connection between language-use and the experience of wholeness is back-stretched, as Herakleitos would say: under tension, like the tips of the archer's bow. As Xiè Língyùn suggests, language cannot *capture* lyric experience. The nature poem's poignancy, its ability to pierce us, derives from this very failure: we are left longing for a wholeness that — awash in chatter or in thrall to analysis — we find hard to come by.

~

The word 'nature' came into the English language almost a thousand years ago. The *Oxford English Dictionary* says it was "adopted from the French *nature* in the 12th Century, an adaptation of the Latin *natura* meaning birth, constitution, character, course of things...."

Its root is the participial stem of *nasci*, to be born. In this range of meanings, it echoes the parallel term in Greek, *phusis*. Of 'nature,' the OED adds that the "native" — that would be *natural* — English word is *kind*. That word has a history that connects it to *kin*, which evolved from a hypothetical Indo-European root, *ǧen*, as in *genus, engender,* and *genesis*. Thus we are brought once again to the notion of origins, and of living patterns that unfold out of them.

Thought of in this way, nature is not merely a collection of undomesticated biomass. Nature is the tendency in things to be what they are, and in that tendency to present themselves as both distinct and connected. To put this another way: If we think of nature as ecology, its 'individuals' are really nothing more than nodes in a huge network — imagine the mathematical points of intersection that define a geodesic dome. Remove any one of these nodes, or pull it out of place, and everything else in the system shifts to accommodate the change. A remarkable interdependence. But the odd thing is, as the analogy with mathematical points makes clear, it leaves the individuals — the mountains, the rivers, the swallows and frogs — ontologically dimensionless. They turn out to be nothing more than sets of *relata*. But what we love when we love a mountain, or a river, or an animal, is nothing so abstract. Still less is it the whole system that, in a sense, expresses itself as the series of relations that define a given node. What we *love,* what love reveals and is disciplined by, is a *this* — a particular and *irreplaceable* entity, that stands out, haloed, against the chaotic backdrop of 'everything else.' And surely, on another view, nature just is the collection of these distinct — loved or feared, rafter-skimming or pond-delving – *things.* Or, rather, it is this *also*. Nature, understood as the tendency in things to be what they are, is the working out of origins through individuals. Its etymology captures the fundamental tension between the wholeness of what-is and the particularity of the beings that, at any moment, exist.

Yet another way of putting this is to say that the nature of nature has the structure of metaphor: something whose meaning arises from incompatible gestalts that, we insist, occupy the same space.

Why do we so insist?

Because we know the paradox shows more than it, or we, can say. Because it points beyond the truths that grammar might deliver up to us, to what is real and unhoused, structurally and constitutionally outside our linguistic grasp.

Because the thinking of being is trued by love of the real.

The Ethics of the Negative Review

The critics killed Keats. What writer has ever had a bad review and not felt the truth of Byron's claim? That squelching of self and creativity. It's one of the reasons that, when I was review editor for *The Fiddlehead* in the early '90s, I made a point of requesting that a review be written only if the reviewer was genuinely enthusiastic about a book. I had other motives, too. One was that I hoped, in this way, to get writing that was *engaged* with its subject matter, and not simply sleepwalking its way to another line in someone's CV. Secondly, as a poet, I was only too aware how many excellent books were published each year to no notice of any sort: it seemed perverse to kill trees to complain about the bad ones. But mostly I thought there was no need to sharpen the hatchets when a deathly critical silence would do all the public work that needed doing. It's this motive on which I wish to dwell because I know my views are not universally shared. I've heard writers say — in defence of a negative review they've given another writer — that they 'had a duty to tell it like it is.' — A duty! The philosopher in me sits up at this suggestion, because it implies that those of us who *don't* do 'our duty' in this regard, or even agitate against doing it, are pursuing a morally degenerate course. So I want to spend a while reflecting on whether or not we *do* have a duty of some sort, at least on occasion, to say publicly that someone has written a bad book. Could it be that Keats's assassins were being better moral citizens than we think?

Some may feel that, in putting the question this way, I'm trying to cheat: we all know Keats belongs in the canon, so whoever thumped *him* shouldn't have. But this objection actually brings me to my first observation: if we're going to accept that we have a *duty* to offer public negative criticism of a work, then, given the potential seriousness of the consequences for the work's creator, we also have a duty to be pretty sure we're right. Many readers now feel that the critics who killed Keats shouldna done what they done done. But at the time, those critics were presumably just saying it like it was — or, at least like it seemed. So the first lesson I want to draw is this: we need to be sure beyond a reasonable doubt, each time we take up the rhetorical cudgels, that our judgement is going to stand the test of time. And frankly, at least in certain cases, I don't think we *can* be sure.

Here, though, a host of questions and objections rears its head. "Wait a minute — are you just *assuming* there's a canon? And on the other hand, are you also suggesting that all critical opinion is merely subjective? Are you trying to tell people they shouldn't express their opinions? And you can't seriously think there aren't ever any bad books — so what're we supposed to do about them? Lie? Besides, really, don't you think ol' Jack was being a bit too sensitive?" Let me take these questions one at a time, because each raises a serious point. And let me add, before I do, that in trying to trace the currents of objection and counter-objection here, I don't mean to be taking a 'me vs. them' stance. Some years ago — it was actually my first journal publication — I wrote a negative review, which I now heartily regret. I make this confession not to try to put the past behind me, but to make it clear that I know, from the inside, where the arguments for negative reviewing come from, and that in my analysis of the issues I'm talking as much to myself as to others.

Defenders of the Faith

The first worry, then — because of my remarks about Keats — is that my argument must be assuming the existence of a canon. Is it? On the contrary. I'm suggesting that it is *the idea that we have a duty to be negative* (once we're sure the book really is a bad book …) that assumes the existence of a canon or at least a standard of excellence. If there were no such standard to uphold, we couldn't be imagining that we owed it to the reading public to tell it that some work or other had failed to measure up. "Well, okay then," the negative reviewer might respond, "who's to say there *isn't* a canon?"

No one. I am, myself, convinced that there is such a thing as great literature — literature whose imaginative depth and energy allow it to span cultures, classes, and epochs. But what's interesting is that *this* belief doesn't entail a duty to trash stuff. Saying there's a duty to denounce failures means there has to be a standard to measure the failures by; but saying there's a standard doesn't, by itself, prove there's a duty to denounce. To prove there's a duty to denounce, you'd have to add that potential misdemeanours are somehow a threat to the standard's existence. ("We must be vigilant!") In other words, even though it might *look* like the existence of the canon is the issue here, it's not. The issue is whether — just supposing for a moment that it exists — any such canon would need a cohort of hit-persons in each generation to maintain its authority. The suggestion strikes me as worse than silly: I think it's incoherent. *Great* literature — as I've defined it and if it exists — couldn't require boundary police to ensure a readership. Its greatness lies precisely in its ongoing ability to move, provoke, and inspire an audience. So, to reiterate, whether or not a canon exists is not actually the issue here. If it doesn't exist, pretending to defend it is just a power grab; and if it does, pretending to defend it is like getting prissy about God — it's going to survive regardless of our efforts to save it or run it out of town.

Some reviewers, especially those who are writers themselves, might agree that it's not really the canon that's at stake, but they'll urge that there's something far more important that is: craft. They believe that if *someone* doesn't take the trouble to point out when publishers, and subsequently readers, are being duped by authors who can't tell a line of iambic pentameter from a clog dance, then the whole business of literature might just end up going to hell in a handcart. Near and dear though craft is to my heart, I think this worry, too, is ultimately a red herring. Writers tend to be self-educators: by flooding the market with bad books, you might conceivably slow down the process by which they come to recognize the importance of craft, but you won't be able to stop them from wondering what's in the library. I have watched too many beginning poets discover Donne, or Bishop, or Moore, or Larkin for themselves to doubt that the capacity to recognize technical virtuosity springs eternal. A reviewer who's really concerned about craft, then, might seek out opportunities to assist in such discoveries; but they'll know that grousing about poorly executed work is usually counterproductive. In literature as in the grade school classroom, it engenders surliness rather than excitement. It also engenders the suspicion that the friends of craft are grumpy, didactic snobs — not true, of course (at least, not true of all of them), but it's a reputation those of us who cherish craft should work to avoid.

I Know What I Like! And Nobody's Going to Tell Me Different

Above, I said I think that —at least in some cases — we can't be sure beyond a reasonable doubt that our critical judgement is going to stand the test of time. How can this be consistent with my view that there really is such a thing as great — or at least good — literature? Am I really saying literary taste is ultimately subjective — that no one can actually tell good books from bad ones? No. Or at least not exactly. What I want to emphasize is that some cases — often those most likely to call forth critical invective (or hyperbolic praise) — are *difficult to decide*. They're cases where the writer is doing something novel, something we're not used to hearing — and *maybe* it's just crap, or *maybe* they're a genius, but it's very hard, with that new and not-fully-savoured taste still in our mouths, to rightly say. To trust an immediate impulse to reject such writing (or an immediate impulse to turn it into a craze) is to consign ourselves to eternal literary childhood, pouting or wailing when we're not offered a certain sort of lollipop. (Or making ourselves insufferable over our infatuation with some New Taste Sensation.) It is to deprive ourselves of one of the signal benefits of learning to read widely: the chance to grow up.

It's a Free Country, Isn't It?

"But what happens if the project isn't novel?" the negative reviewer now objects. "What if it is, indeed, the same old same old and, as all your friends and even your enemies are saying — in private — badly done to boot? Why shouldn't a person express their opinion? It's a free country — at least it's supposed to be. What's wrong with saying what you think?" This argument is interesting, in part because it shifts the ground of debate away from the performance of a duty to the exercise of a privilege. Now the negative reviewer is not saying they *ought* to say a book is bad; they're saying something weaker — that they have a *right* to say it's bad if they want to. I'll return to this point in a moment. First, I want to focus on another feature of this response: that it assumes all expression of 'opinion' is like the expression of political opinion.

Here's the negative reviewer's argument: "If I say, publicly, 'Buying TMX with taxpayers' money was criminal as well as stupid!', I don't expect Justin Trudeau to quit politics because I've spoken my mind and my view is different from his. So if I say, 'I don't think Q should have published this book!,' what's the difference?" But this, I think, importantly misconstrues the analogy with reviewing. Debate is indeed a crucial part of politics in a democratic society — and this means one needs to be tolerant, and also able to take one's knocks in the political arena. But theses and arguments — the *stuff* of politics — are rarely the building materials of artistic insight; and opinions about theses and arguments are qualitatively different from opinions about artistic achievement. For one thing, there is no culture of 'equal time for the opposition.' Writers who've been attacked are not encouraged to 'get in there' and defend their work. They are in fact encouraged to 'rise above it' — advice that would make no sense in a political context unless the attack were pointedly and pointlessly personal.

Another indication that political success and artistic merit don't occupy the same arena is that it is possible to be appalled by a writer's politics and nonetheless respect, admire, even be attracted to, their work as art. (Philip Larkin would be an example in my case.) Yes, art can *be* intensely political, both in the sense of giving expression to a political ethos and in the sense of being riddled by politics. And where a work of literature gives expression to political views, or where its reception is clearly being affected by the political views of its readers, those views might well be made the subject of public debate. So, for example, we might want to discuss, as *politics,* the class snobbery that appears to have informed John Lockhart's vicious review of *Endymion*. But to say "Lockhart was an elitist" isn't to say "Lockhart couldn't write." That is: in many cases, we can tell the difference between a person's politics and their artistic ability. There are indeed huge questions about the relation of rhetoric to meaning, about the political dimensions of every communicative gesture. But to acknowledge this does not mean it makes sense to bring the rhetorical style of the campaign trail into every encounter. Pounding a writer in print for their lack of talent is not good reviewing practice *just because* it's an exercise in free speech. To suggest it is is to miss ways in which art and politics can in fact be distinguished.

I'd like to turn now to the argumentative shift from performing a duty ("Negative reviews *ought* to be written") to the exercise of a privilege ("I have a right to say whatever I want"). Apart from the fact that this argument no longer makes negative reviewing a duty, two things are worth noting. The first is that, while we may indeed have a right to say whatever we want, we often choose not to exercise it. (It may, in truth, be your opinion that the hairstyle of the person sitting next to you on the bus looks ridiculous. Do you stand up in the aisle and pronounce your verdict? Why not?) The second is that the ideal we're appealing to is one in which individuals are also quite clear that the opinions are *theirs*: political debate (at least ideally) is conducted in the first person. A great deal of negative reviewing, on the other hand, is conducted in the amorphous non-person favoured by departments of English — as though eschewing the word 'I' might actually relieve the writer of a merely human perspective on the universe. What it achieves, of course, is nothing of the sort: it produces needlessly cumbersome constructions and the illusion of authority. In my experience, frequent and explicit use of the first person produces, by contrast, a 'situated' voice. (Unless, of course, the 'I' is always in italics — "*I* think ..." — in which case the sneer quotient can reach unbearable proportions.) Where it's not in italics, the use of 'I' focalizes the reviewer; it allows the question "Who are you to be saying this?" to cross the reader's mind, and, with it, the thought that the reader's own view might be different.

Does this mean I think negative reviewing would be acceptable if only it were written in the first person? No. It's just that I think what's problematic about it would be more easily discerned.

What about Bad Books?

But first, let me return to one of the most pressing questions surrounding the practice of negative reviewing: What do we do about bad books? (Or books that we think are bad.) Am I suggesting we're supposed to *lie* about them? Disown our considered judgements? Indeed not. I am suggesting simply that, in public, we keep our mouths shut. "But isn't that hypocritical?" the critic will ask. "Isn't it *dishonest*?" — It's dishonest only if one has been asked a direct question *and* knows silence is likely to be taken for praise. But, of course, neither of these conditions usually obtains. Most reviewers who write for literary periodicals are given some choice; and I cannot think of a case where, in print, a reviewer has been asked to respond to the question: "Oh, don't you think Q's new book is just *lovely*? I just think it's *lovely*! Don't you think it's *lovely*?" (— in response to which, it's conceivable, silence might be mistaken for assent). Often, reviewers can negotiate the books they are going to review — at least within limits; and frequently enough, the space taken up by a negative review precludes any notice being given to a book the reviewer likes. This, I think, harms the reading public instead of serving it. It's not as though readers who are warned off will then rush out and order books they don't even know exist. Most small-press Canadian poetry, for example, doesn't even show up on the shelves of most Canadian bookstores.

"Ah! *That's* your problem!" the response may come. "You're thinking about all this in terms of that non-market genre, poetry. But what about *fiction*? Big money to be made there. What about authors with big reps whose bad books would otherwise be bought by the shelfful just because of the name on the spine? And don't you think it's unfair that Q gets all the money and gigs when P writes better books?"

Sure it's unfair; but I don't think reviewers should take it upon themselves to right such wrongs by slinging invective at Q's work. Far more effective to use the column space to draw attention to the great stuff P has been producing. And I think reviewers are just kidding themselves if they imagine dumping on a famous novelist is actually going to crimp sales. (As far as *publicists* are concerned, any review is a good review.) Again, the reviewer who's feeling truly spiteful could probably do much more damage by drawing the public's attention to Moderately-Well-Known Author P and saying almost nothing about Famous Author Q, than by fuming about Q in public.

"But you're still not getting it," the negative reviewer will sigh. "If you've got a gig writing a review column for some paper, there are books you just can't ignore. If you don't review Famous Author Q's new book (or New and Much-Hyped First Author X's), you're out of a job because your editor knows readers will switch to the paper that *does* review it. And, let's face it, review readers sometimes like it a little rough. That sells papers, too."

— Well, now we're getting down to it, aren't we? This reply has, I think, a great deal of credibility. But notice it says nothing about a reviewer's duty, or even their rights. It says that publishing — at least the publishing of mass market fiction and journalistic nonfiction — is just another market enterprise, and as such is subject to the perversions with which market capitalism has made us only too familiar. Here, then, I have no quarrel with the negative reviewer: if the claim is that in order to supplement a meagre income a struggling writer is sometimes forced by the system to review a book that should be ignored, and to review it in a way that serves no genuine literary purpose, then, it seems to me, the negative reviewer is probably telling it like it is. The question now becomes: is there an alternative?

The Art of the Review

Look at the word itself: *re-view*. To take a second look; or a third. To look again. But to what purpose? The *Oxford English Dictionary* suggests it's often "with a view to correction or improvement." That's an effortful version of the style we've been considering: "this is wrong and this is wrong and this is wrong, and here, Q, is what you should have done...." The OED does offer us another perspective, though, in a later definition: the aim of the second look can be to further "appreciation." The reviewer who understands their task in these terms, then, would be one who has taken the trouble to listen again, to listen with care, curiosity, and respect, in an attempt to give genuine attention to what is being said. And who can assist the rest of us begin to listen attentively, too. This is a portrait of the reviewer as a kind of literary naturalist, someone with sharp ears and a good memory, who's willing to tarry alongside both us and the literary world, for whom any item is of potential interest (some less, some more, to be sure), and who, instead of seeing an award culture's hierarchy of achievement, hears a living chorus of voices, talking, murmuring, singing to themselves and to others.

There will be voices any such reviewer will prefer not to dwell on, as poor exemplars or as diseased. Such a reviewer may also be called to speak out against depredations that are deforming an ecosystem or threatening the health of certain species. And they will have to earn a living: sometimes by means that, given the context of global corporate capitalism, will involve doing things that go against their conscience. But they will be *trying*, at all times, to do their best to cultivate the appreciation of books and of literature in general, to help the rest of us listen with enthusiasm, delight, puzzlement, and insight.

Given market pressures, what is the chance we might find our way to the general practice of appreciative reviewing? I think the outlook is not as grim as some might think. There are whole books of such criticism by writers like Helen Vendler, Robert Hass, and, here in Canada, Stan Dragland, which show just how much can be done in this genre. Historically, Virginia Woolf provides us with some excellent examples. There is also the gesture that Dragland made in founding the review journal *Brick*, which took as its motto Rilke's claim: "Works of art are of an infinite loneliness and with nothing to be so little appreciated as with criticism. Only love can grasp and hold them and be just to them." The discipline of the appreciative review is, I believe, among the great unsung arts of our culture. I suspect it remains unsung because, appearances to the contrary, it is not actually a species of *speaking*, but a species of *listening*; and our culture tends to regard listening as neither interesting nor praiseworthy. But listening — real listening — requires that we give over our attention fully to the other, that we stop worrying about who's noticing us, that we let the ego go. As such, it is an activity requiring much more effort than the activity of proclaiming our selves through speaking our views. For we are a culture, perhaps a species, drunk on a narrow notion of assertiveness and virility. We are also a culture, and indeed a species, that is highly alert to rank — to the extent that knowing one is on the bottom rung can be felt to be preferable to there being no rungs at all. These twin addictions, as visible in the contemporary university as in the military, lead us to dismiss those with a gift for listening as 'soft,' and to celebrate those with a taste for volubly dispensing judgement as 'tough.' My suggestion is that it is those who nonetheless insist on listening who are really tough: they have the courage to continue to serve art when everything around them is making it easy not to.

In some ways, reviewing is not unlike talking to a friend. There are two dimensions in particular that I'd like to touch on. The first is the degree to which both friends and artists must make themselves *vulnerable* to our critical judgement. Thin skin can mean a couple of things. As prickliness, it is a social liability in politics or the workplace; as sensitivity, however, it is a necessity in both friendship and art. To *be* a friend, to *be* an artist, one must be willing to lay oneself open to some extent: one must be receptive, tuned to the play of emotion and perception, rather than one's own defence. The analogy breaks down in that the artist must be open to the world in general, not to the reviewer in particular — the reviewer enters as a third party, as it were. But the artist's position, I believe, must still be construed as one of trust, one that requires of reviewers respect for the thin skin that is essential to creativity.

The second point of connection concerns how we — friends and reviewers — need to feel if our relationships are to flourish. In friendship, we refrain from making harshly negative comments about our friends as a matter of course. This is not only because we're afraid they'll stop liking us if we're nasty or because we might be squeamish about hurting their feelings. Rather, we are motivated by genuine delight in our friends' well-being. We are engaged by, and with, our friends' virtues — those excellences which, on second, third, and fourth acquaintance, we have come to appreciate, and which we hope others will come to appreciate, too. These are what we will attend to, and what we will speak of — when called to speak. The same, I believe, holds for the relationships with books which are the foundation of an appreciative review. It's what Rilke said: in art, as in friendship, the ear of love discerns more, and more truly, than the eye of judgement.

Integrity and Ornament

> *The work of art wants to tear men out of their comfortable existence.*
> — ADOLF LOOS

In "Ornament and Crime," his famous and famously notorious essay of 1908, Adolf Loos argues that the Hapsburg Viennese love of decorative ornament is morally decadent.

Loos's elaboration of this view is imbued with progress mythology and appears to be racist, as well as sentimental about class hierarchies. He argues that ornament cannot be generated by those who live on "our cultural level"; as examples of those who do not live on that level, he offers "the Papuan" and "the negro," as well as cultural "laggards" in Austria, such as Tyrolean peasants. He describes the reformed style that he advocates as that of "aristocrats."

There is, however, a second strain in Loos's rejection of ornament, one that does not appeal to progress, race, or class.

For Loos, in this second mood, the meaning of a tool or domestic space is its use.

> ADOLF LOOS: We do not sit in such-and-such a way, because a table maker has built a chair in such-and-such a way; rather the table maker makes the chair as he does, because someone wants to sit that way.

This is not Bauhaus, which intends to produce forms that can accommodate any function. Loos does not reject detailing: every design is adapted to a very specific use. He believes that a focus on function in domestic aesthetics leaves no *conceptual* room for ornament.

Are the two strains in Loos's thought — the socio-evolutionary and the functional —connected? He himself writes as though they mutually imply one another. It is my impression, however, that his socio-evolutionary views serve as a secondary interpretive structure for the intuitions that ground the functional strain.

It is not my intention to explore that hypothesis here. I wish instead to explore a possibility opened by the hypothesis: that, whatever their relation in Loos's own thought, there is a way of understanding the functional strain that does not imply racism, class hierarchies, or progress mythology.

The view I will propose rejects ornament as a failure of lyric integration. It rests on an extension of Loos's notion of culturally organic form.

～

What reasons — apart from the preservation of Eurocentric 'master narratives' — might one have for thinking the meaning of domestic objects is given in their use?

> EGON FRIEDELL: These rooms of theirs were not living-rooms, but pawnshops and curiosity-shops[:] ... Rococo mirrors in several pieces, multi-coloured Venetian glass, fat-bellied Old German pots, a skin rug on the floor, complete with terrifying jaws, and, in the hall, a life-sized wooden Negro.... Through it all, the taste for ornament and polychrome made itself felt. The more twists and scrolls and arabesques there were in the designs, the louder and cruder the colour, the greater the success. In connexion with this there is a conspicuous absence of any idea of usefulness or purpose; it was all purely for show.

"Grecian Vase" Toilet,
J.L. Mott Ironworks, 1897

In *Wittgenstein's Vienna,* Allan Janik and Stephen Toulmin argue persuasively that the *éminence grise* — or, more aptly perhaps, *éminence satirique* — behind Loos's condemnation of ornament was Karl Kraus.

Kraus was a polemicist who levelled his attacks at writers and composers whose work catered opportunistically to the tastes of the Hapsburg Viennese — their love of spectacle, titillation, and shallow charm.

> KARL KRAUS: Adolf Loos and I, he literally and I grammatically, have done nothing more than show that there is a distinction between an urn and a chamber pot and that it is this distinction above all that gives culture room to change and develop.

People behaved as though humans were not the animals they are: chamber pots disguised as Greek vases; regular visits to brothels advertised in the newspaper's back pages papered over on page 2 with sanctimonious letters to the editor deploring sex work. They behaved as if the essence of the good life was distraction through meaningless acquisition: the existential emptiness of the bourgeois and upper classes fronted by *art nouveau* clutter.

> EGON FRIEDELL: This brings us to one of the main features of the times: delight in the unreal. Every material used tries to look like more than it is.... Whitewashed tin masquerades as marble, papier mâché as rosewood, plaster as gleaming alabaster, glass as costly onyx.... The sideboard boasts copper vessels, never used for cooking.... On the wall hang defiant swords, never crossed, and proud hunting trophies, never won.... The butter-knife is a Turkish dagger, the ash-tray a Prussian helmet, the umbrella-stand a knight in armour, and the thermometer a pistol.... The beer-jug is a monk, made to open, who is guillotined at every gulp; the clock is an instructive model of an express engine, a glass dachshund serves as cruet for the roast, the salt sneezes, and the gravy is

drawn from a miniature barrel, carried by a nice little terracotta donkey.

~

Loos suggests that ornament that is not "organically bound up with" a culture is not an expression of that culture. What would ornament that *is* organically bound up with a culture amount to?

One possibility is that it would be ornament that grew out of, expressed, maintained, and was maintained by a form of life.

But doesn't the late nineteenth- and early twentieth-century Viennese pursuit of ornament do precisely this — express and maintain a form of life? The Krausian complaint is that the aesthetic dimension of Hapsburg style *reflects* a lack of moral integrity: that the *culture* is dis-integrated.

This suggests that, in addition to maintaining and being maintained by a form of life, culturally organic ornament is possible only to the extent that the form of life to which it gives expression is itself integrated — 'organic' in a sense that derives from healthy living organisms.

What distinguishes a biological being from, say, a mechanical being is an *integration* of parts that is not merely additive. A biological being is an ecology; a machine is the sum of its parts.

In some bio-cultural contexts, what at first sight appears to be ornament is correlated with higher success rates in mating or reproduction, or higher status in a dominance hierarchy. We might think of the plumage of the male ribbon-tailed astrapia, the intensely coloured nectar guides of some flowers, or human fashions in clothing (the codpiece, the bustle). When it comes to sex and status, the line between ornament and functional detail is not sharp. In some cases, it may not exist.

To talk of a dis-integrated *form of life* is to talk of a 'form' that exists only abstractly — as an idea, a commitment to dis-integrated expression in ways of living, grasped through language. Such a 'form' is not a structure perceived through the exercise of gestalt intelligence, a kind of intelligence that has been fundamental to both functional design and art in many cultures. A dis-integrated style pushes back against gestalt intelligence; it says such perception is irrelevant.

≈

Integrity is an ecological concept. It names a particular kind of wholeness: one in which every aspect of a complex entity contributes to the stability of the whole, and to the well-being of every other aspect. Integrity stands to the aspects that it integrates as a gestalt stands to the sub-gestalts that it embraces: the whole is ontologically dependent on the parts, and yet the full meanings of those parts are indiscernible independently of the whole in which they live.

This sort of wholeness is defining of forms that we intuitively recognize as lyric.

In lyric form, so-called details — aspects, parts, constitutive gestures — are not details in a structural sense. There is no metaphysically distinct essence to which they are mere adjuncts. In lyric form, 'essence' *is* the living network of constitutive 'detail.'

That is, aesthetic integrity is a fundamental characteristic of lyric works in any medium.

To say that there is a connection between aesthetic and moral integrity is to say that aesthetic integrity consists of, rests on, sensitivity to and honesty about who we are and what we perceive.

As we learn more about perception, we learn that 'sense organs' do not passively register 'sense data' which is then transmitted to the brain where it is converted to 'information' about 'what's out there.' Rather, cognition (as it is called) frequently structures and anticipates perception; facilitates it; hinders it. Attention plays a crucial role, and is mediated by numerous factors.

In addition, there are more things and more intelligences in the cosmos than are dreamt of in most analytic philosophy departments.

To perceive well, to perceive honestly, requires the exercise of discernment.

To say there is a connection between aesthetic and moral integrity is to say: meaning should, if possible, be clear.

If meaning for domestic objects is use, their use must not be disguised.

≈

In many respects, Hapsburg Vienneses style resembles some among the styles that we have come to call postmodern.

> CALL FOR SUBMISSIONS, *CRIME AND ORNAMENT*, OFFERING A CHARACTERIZATION OF POSTMODERNISM: It is a product of late capitalism ... [it] appropriates, commodifies, fragments the past ... [and] cannibalizes other cultures.... [T]he past [along with other cultures] is rendered as mere spectacle, ... pastiche and nostalgia.

Yet many postmodern critics would agree that hypocrisy is a bad thing. In some sense, that's what postmodernism is about — deconstructing the hypocrisy of so-called master narratives' claims to truth. If postmodernism rejects hypocrisy, though, why do some versions of it also appear to reject integrity?

One possibility is that the idea that there is a connection between moral and aesthetic integrity is one of the 'master narratives' that needs to be deconstructed.

Another possibility is that, to the extent that postmodernism resists a connection between moral and aesthetic integrity, it is itself an expression of the same 'master narrative' that it claims to be transcending.

~

Some advocates of postmodernism describe their project as the 'undoing' of the 'hierarchical binary' 'essence *vs.* accident' (or, as the postmodernism in question sometimes characterizes it, 'essence *vs.* excess').

In practice, however, there is tension between this ideal and at least some works that purport to embody it.

For the collapse of ornamental function — a *genuine* erasure of the distinction between essence and accident — points to a particular, classical, conception of style, *viz.*, lyric.

In lyric style, as in Loosian domestic design, the distinction between essence and accident makes no sense: everything is essence because the whole is the living network of its interdependent particulars.

Yet artists in the European tradition whose work is driven by intuitions of lyric coherence — Praxiteles, Johannes Vermeer, Anselm Kiefer — are viewed by some postmodern critics as members of a canon we must reject. We must be suspicious of their work not only because they are dead white males but because coherence itself is suspect: its pursuit belongs to one of the master narratives that must be overcome. "Beauty," that is, lyric integrity, "is boring." Incoherence of the Hapsburg Viennese sort is fun.

This suggests that there is a version of postmodernism that wants ornament *to be ornament* while denying that there is anything structurally 'necessary' that it is ornamenting. But if there were *only* ornament, that one thing, *by definition,* could not be ornament.

In other words, a celebration of ornament *as* ornament cannot involve the undoing of hierarchical binaries. A celebration of ornament *as* ornament has simply reversed the emphasis in the hierarchical binary 'essence *vs.* accident.'

We would, if we were trying to engage in such a celebration coherently, have to underline the paradoxical nature of our speech, or find expressions that didn't appeal to the vocabulary of ornament and thus imply the dualism on which such vocabulary rests.

A reversal of emphasis in a given hierarchical binary may have important political aims. It may be a pointed way of calling attention to a lack of non-circular justification for the emphasis it opposes. But that, of course, is less radical than an attempt to eliminate the hierarchy in the binary altogether or, most radical of all, to pursue a non-binary way of thinking.

Is it possible to have experience that is not structured according to binaries? If so, is it then possible to express that experience without appealing to binaries? These questions are complex and their exploration would take us far afield.

It is possible, however, to minimize the endorsement one's expression gives to certain grand metaphysical hierarchies such as form and content, essence and accident, substance and particular. The refusal of these hierarchies is fundamental to lyric thought in any medium.

And now we begin to see why lyric integration is profoundly opposed by some versions of postmodernism: *some* of the work that flies under the postmodern banner depends on a *dis*integration of elements to achieve its political purpose. By celebrating ornament as ornament, it insists, however covertly, on a metaphysically distinct 'basic' structure that is ornamented. This is a politics that wants the world order to be roughly what it already is except that those on the bottom and the top switch places. Its emotional colour is often vengeful and self-focussed; for this reason, its creativity can be circumscribed. Its vision must be short-term, for the wheel of Fortune does not cease to turn.

A postmodern style that wishes to celebrate ornament in good faith must — and in some quarters, does — do so in a clear awareness of its continuity with European thought of the last two thousand years. In particular, it is aware of its acceptance of canonical metaphysical distinctions.

A critique that aims coherently to undo those distinctions must also admit its continuity with the past. Lyric has always been radical; that is, it has always been one of art's roots.

~

Art, Loos claimed, is functionless; and because functionless, not subject to the imperatives imposed on design by the view that meaning, for domestic objects and spaces, is use. Function-sensitive design, he believed, has nothing to do with art precisely because it concerns objects and activities essential to our form of life.

> ADOLF LOOS: The house has to please everyone. To distinguish it from art, which does not have to please anyone.... The work of art is set into the world without there being any need for it. The house satisfies a need.... The work of art wants to tear men out of their comfortable existence. The house must serve their comfort.... *So the house would have nothing to do with art, and architecture shouldn't be classified under the arts? It is so.* Only a very small part of architecture belongs to art: the tomb and the monument. The rest, everything that serves a purpose, is to be excluded from the realm of art.

Lyric style can embrace forms produced by function-sensitive design. It is also fundamental to a good deal of what many cultures recognize as art.

Lyric style is thus a wider notion than either Loos's notion of function-sensitive design or his notion of art.

Loos was not opposed to ornament in art. He was opposed to the conflation of art and domestic design. His own argument for that position appealed to a socio-evolutionary view that many of us find objectionable. But such arguments are not needed for suggesting that there is something suspect about disguising toilets as Greek vases.

One objection to such ornamentation is that the disguise involves a form of hypocrisy: the pretense that shit is not different from flowers. Another objection is that it is incoherent — culturally, historically, and as a matter of fact. The Hapsburg Viennese did not live in ancient Greece; there is no indication in the archaeological record that the ancient Greeks themselves disguised chamber pots as vases; toilets are not vases any more than fossil fuel corporations are good environmental citizens.

Are such hypocrisy and incoherence serious crimes? Perhaps not. But if we acquiesce in them, if we regard them as a kind of fun-without-consequences, we are allowing that at least in some circumstances truth does not matter. If it does not matter, then why care about deconstructing 'master narratives'? Or racism, or class hierarchies, or progress mythology?

Who cares about truth? I do.

A self-aware postmodern style that emphasizes ornament over 'essential' form for the purposes of exposing false consciousness shares this aim with at least some versions of a functional critique of ornament.

To summarize:
   A postmodernism that celebrates ornament as ornament while claiming it is undoing hierarchical binaries deludes itself.

An undeluded postmodernism that celebrates ornament as ornament cannot do so without acknowledging its continuity with canonical Western European metaphysics, particularly its reliance on the ancient distinction between essence and accident, or that between core material and detail.

A postmodernism that genuinely attempts to undo hierarchical binaries stands in solidarity with lyric thought throughout human history and culture, including the lyric intuitions that generated much of what we understand as high modernism in English literature (if not American architecture).

To celebrate and glorify frivolousness and hypocrisy on a cultural scale is one way of embodying decadence.

Only by admitting its decadence, then, can we view a postmodernism that engages in such celebration as revolutionary.

A non-decadent postmodernism accepts at least some of the core distinctions of Western European metaphysics, or it is continuous with the way of thinking that has sought constantly to undo those metaphysics.

> HERAKLEITOS: *Into the same rivers we step and do not step; we are and are not.*

The Novels of Pascal: A Review of *Correction* by Thomas Bernhard

After a particularly severe intestinal infection, so called, which against all expectation had laid me up for several days, confining me first to bed and later, as my strength began to return, to the house, for the weather, so called, had by then turned cold and was unsuitable for physical exercise of any sort, even physical exercise by the healthy, those *outwardly unaffected* in body or spirit, in the subsequent state of convalescence, after the most extreme manifestations of the illness were past, I took up the matter that I had laid aside some months previously, having been detained by our neighbour's court appearance on charges of assault and battery, a case of unusual and unaccountable violence, the matter of the review of Krankheit's novel surrounding the life and work of the so-called greatest of this century's Austrian philosophers, about whom, of course, some of my own previous writings, so called, had centred. The infection had been of the most virulent kind, attacking all aspects of my so-called being with extreme and astonishing force, so that even now its debilitating effects could be felt, particularly in the way of certain mental perturbations, which had been most pronounced at the time. Notwithstanding, I had determined to pursue this project, the project of the review of *Corruption*, which had been handed on to me, passed down the line, so to speak, as would have been apparent even to the least incurious by examination of the volume's *flyleaf* upon which, with absolutely no attempt at legibility, had been inscribed the names of all its previous owners, all writers, every one of them, every one a prospective reviewer, without exception persons of the utmost artistic integrity and gifted with extraordinary powers of discrimination, who had nonetheless declined or had not felt called to undertake this project, the project on which I was now about to embark, of writing down, *in the most accurate way possible,* those thoughts and feelings that had possessed me on reading Krankheit's work, not only this volume but also the numerous other volumes, the so-called novels and autobiographical novels, which had established his reputation at the forefront of European letters. This reading, of course, given the limitations of my acquaintance with German, had been wholly and in every respect confined to *the reading of translated texts,* texts, therefore, that it became doubly difficult to assess, seeing, as I was, not only through the eyes of Krankheit himself, but through those of his translators, who are after all *interpreters,* those least likely in the end to have had any regard for the essential uninterpretability of his experience, indeed of any experience whatsoever of whatever person however expressed and however apparently interpretable on the surface, so that this task that I had taken on, of *interpreting* the work of Krankheit to others, articulating in a coherent fashion the basic principles and tenets of his thought, a task that on the so-called surface might not appear particularly difficult, might even, on the so-called surface, appear to be easy, on further reflection, the more I read the works, the so-called novels and autobiographical novels, and the deeper my acquaintance with them became, the more it seemed that the difficulty of the task grew, in the most unexpected manner, *precisely in inverse proportion* to my familiarity with the works, thus, what had once seemed the easiest, the least troublesome of undertakings, came to seem the most difficult of undertakings, a matter of vast and impenetrable complexity that even now I am tempted to speak of as *wholly and completely impossible.* This sense was not least of all owing to the necessity imposed on me from the first and continuing to impose itself at every moment thereafter of making some sense of the relation between Krankheit's so-called style, itself of the most individual and remarkable stamp, and the *content,* not only the content of this volume, with its title at once highly suggestive and indeterminate, but also the content of *every other volume,* the so-called novels and autobiographical novels, each with its own title and executed in an equally individual and remarkable manner, to much the same effect as far as I could tell with my limited knowledge of German and the limitations thereby imposed on me by my necessary and unavoidable reliance on translators, those least likely to be concerned with the peculiar difficulties of a reviewer in relation to the task at hand, difficulties that were beginning to appear to be virtually insurmountable. It was in just this way that Krankheit himself saw, *or appeared to see,* life itself (so called): a series of appalling and incomprehensible acts of criminal violence. We are surrounded *on every side* by stupidity and idiocy, by disease and corruption which, if correctly perceived, inevitably produces an overwhelming preoccupation with suicide, the act of complete eradication which is the only plausible response to the intolerable conditions that life imposes on each one of us, the final correction. Speaking of the condition of those who have chosen to marry, Krankheit wrote, "At first we hear nothing unusual from all these people, if we do hear something about them, and then we hear only revolting things, *only revolting things,*" so Krankheit, "only revolting things" in italics, "just as, in our own case, we see nothing unusual in our parents at first, but later we see only revolting things. Nature is that incomprehensible force that brings people together, forcibly pushes them together, by every means, so that these people will destroy themselves, annihilate, kill, ruin, extinguish themselves," so Krankheit. "Then they throw themselves down a rock cleft, or off a bridge railing, or they shoot themselves, like my uncle, or they hang themselves, like my other uncle, or they throw themselves in front of a train, like my third uncle," so Krankheit, all in the character of one Roithamer, a person of prodigious talents and obsessive preoccupations, bearing many superficial and characterological resemblances to a well-known Austrian philosopher, though it was Wittgenstein's *brothers* who all killed themselves, and not by hanging or throwing themselves in front of trains. There is another novel, so called, by Krankheit which, had it been translated at the time, which it hadn't, the reasons for this remaining entirely obscure and unavailable to the so-called novel-reading public in North America, we were being kept entirely in the dark, would have appeared on our bookshelves as, in all likelihood, *Wittgenstein's Nephew.* This fact, the fact of this novel's existence, clearly could serve only to reinforce the significance of Krankheit's depiction of relations of consanguinity here in *Corruption,* relations concerning which *everything* may be at stake, on which our understanding of Krankheit's entire œuvre may hinge, though what that significance is remains at the moment highly conjectural, remains, in fact, entirely open to speculation. "We ourselves are the most suicide *prone*," this character of Krankheit's goes on, "prone" in italics, "and didn't our cousin, the only son of our third uncle, kill himself too, after he got married to a doctor's daughter from Kirchdorf on the Krems, a marriage that simply couldn't have worked out," so Krankheit's protagonist, Roithamer, "that *handsome man,*" so the protagonist, "handsome man" in italics, "who threw himself into a cleft in the rock in the Tennen Mountains, over a thousand meters down into a dark cleft in the rock. Because I wanted to see how deep that cleft in the rock was, I once made a detour on my way home from England to Altensam to this rock cleft in the Tennen Mountains, I went climbing up those high mountains in a constant and worsening state of vertiginous nausea, putting the utmost strain on my physical resources as I'm not cut out by nature for climbing high mountains, and I actually made it to that cleft in the rock and I looked down into that cleft because I couldn't believe that so deep a cleft in the rock could exist, but that cleft is even much deeper; so it was here, into this very cleft in the rock that my cousin threw himself, I thought, standing at its rim and looking down into its depths and for a moment I was tempted to throw myself into that cleft too, but suddenly, when this idea was at its most compelling, this idea seemed ridiculous to me, and I took myself out of there," so Krankheit's protagonist. The only recourse, Krankheit seems to be suggesting, is to pull away from society completely, from the norms that society imposes, norms that after all are only the expression of an essentially base and criminal nature capable of the most *incomprehensible and disgusting acts of violence,* thus Krankheit, so that if one is to escape from this condition, this so-called state of affairs, one must pursue a life of *complete and rigorous* solitude, so Krankheit's works might suggest, a life like that of central, suicidal characters in all Krankheit's so-called novels and autobiographical novels. Even so, there remains one factor in which these characters, these *men,* all of whom, including Krankheit himself as he assures us in the autobiographical novels, are men of the most extraordinary brilliance and genius, capable of almost unimaginable acts of imagination and existential courage, these men are nevertheless less than wholly isolate in that each one of them lives with, or is taken care of by, or, as in this novel, *Corruption,* is wholly preoccupied with, his sister, a woman who in each instance never appears as a person of a fully determinate nature, but as a shadowy and silent figure, often insane or appearing otherwise ill, whose entire being is taken up with ministering to the needs of her brother, including, either by innuendo or direct statement, needs of a sexual nature. Then there are the birds, the murdered birds, originally living birds of rare and exotic species who, by some mechanism or mechanisms unknown, have arrived in the gorges in which so many of Krankheit's characters find themselves, as for example the narrator, not Roithamer but a character who is following in Roithamer's footsteps, Roithamer having spent most of his final days in a garret in the home of Hoeller where the narrator now is staying. "Suddenly I heard the Aurach," writes Krankheit in the character of the narrator, "and I thought how all this time I'd believed there was a perfect silence in Hoeller's family room, while in fact one always hears the roaring Aurach here, even though I had grown so accustomed to the incessant noise, especially loud at this particular spot in the Aurach gorge, that after a certain point I had ceased to notice it, so that I believed, while actually surrounded by the thunderous roar of the Aurach in the Aurach gorge, that here was perfect quiet, because I no longer heard the incessant roar of the Aurach, just as the Hoellers no longer hear it, except once in a while, when they suddenly become aware of it again, they hear it all the time without a break and because of that they no longer hear it, only for moments, when they think of it just as I had ceased to hear it, although the most striking feature of the Hoeller house is undoubtedly the roaring of the

Aurach, the arriving and the arrived are totally enclosed in this roar, actually it is always hard to communicate with those who live there, one has to scream to be heard, yet everyone gets used to it very quickly, probably because the Aurach roar is so deafening, and then it may be quite soon that one perceives as perfect stillness what is actually in uproar, as I have just experienced it myself." So Krankheit writes in *Corruption,* although it is an entirely characteristic passage, both in form and content, and might easily have come from any one of a number of other pieces he has written. As for birds, what Krankheit has written in this novel is also entirely characteristic of what he has written in other novels. "By stuffing this bird," he says in one passage, "he is making the night bearable for himself. At twelve," the passage continues, the speaker in this case again being the narrator, who is observing his host Hoeller from his (the narrator's) post in Hoeller's garret, "at twelve, he was still busy stuffing that bird. Off and on I kept wondering what kind of a bird this was, I'd never seen so large and so black a bird before, probably a species never seen in our country at all, and I toyed with the idea of going down to the workshop to ask Hoeller what species of bird this was. It's certainly possible that this bird is of a so-called exotic species," so Krankheit's narrator, "a species that one of the hunters living out there on the plain, living in affluence in that fertile country out there, men who take frequent hunting trips to foreign countries and overseas, brought the bird back from South America or Africa, with what incredible energy Hoeller was now stuffing that bird with polyurethane, I couldn't imagine that so much polyurethane could be crammed inside that bird, yet Hoeller kept stuffing some of the polyurethane into the bird, suddenly I felt repelled by the process of stuffing polyurethane into the huge black bird, I turned around, looked at the door, but found it impossible to look at the door for more than a second or so because even looking at the door I kept seeing the huge bird Hoeller was stuffing with polyurethane, so I turned back again and looked out the window and into Hoeller's workshop, if I must see Hoeller stuff this huge, black, really horrible bird, then I might as well see it in reality and not in my imagination, clearly I could not possibly expect to get any sleep now, full as I was of my impression of Hoeller stuffing that huge black bird with polyurethane, constantly accelerating the speed with which he was doing this job, it was nauseating, still I had to keep looking out the window and into the workshop as if hypnotized. I could no longer turn away, compelled to surrender myself entirely to watching this procedure of Hoeller's cramming that bird with polyurethane, I was about to vomit when Hoeller suddenly stopped his horrible activity and set the bird down, with its huge claws and long heavy legs, on his worktable." So Krankheit in *Corruption*. Exotic murdered birds and roaring water, the roaring waters of a gorge, a steep cleft, the mysterious sister, the silent other half that slips in and out of doors in the whitewashed rooms of the self-made prisons of Krankheit's protagonists, including prisons situated in forests, forests the protagonist has made silent by executing all the living creatures within their bounds, in which the protagonist works on his great work, thus Krankheit, a work of the utmost difficulty requiring the most strenuous mental effort, and which, in the end, "might possibly boil down to a single thought," so the industrialist in *Grotesqueries*, which could also have been called *Dérangement* if its title had been translated literally into English, a thought which, were it achieved, I find myself speculating, would perhaps finally open the doors to suicide, doors that, despite the tremendous pressure placed upon them, remain resolutely closed whilst the protagonist pursues his agonizing task, a task essentially of self-elimination. But what, then, with these recurring motifs, the motifs of the birds, the sister, the gorge, and above all the motif of suicide, and indeed also, the *motif of the style itself,* the style in its motivic configuration, what, then, has this particular volume, this volume as distinct from all the other volumes, the novels and so-called autobiographical novels, also by Krankheit, all possessing the same motivic preoccupations, what has this novel in particular to do with Wittgenstein, preoccupied though he was with perfection and suicide, whatever his penchant for isolation and plain interiors, whatever his undoubted fondness for his sisters and his tendency to underline words? "Basically we have here a people given to constant discussion of its own suicide," so writes Krankheit in *Corruption,* "a people which at the same time is constantly having to prevent itself from committing suicide, this is as true of each individual as of the population as a whole, they're always at it, singly and collectively, and what it actually amounts to is a state of incessant suffering made bearable, however, by the high intelligence applied to it by each individual and therefore by the people as a whole. It's a folk art of sorts," so the narrator to Hoeller, "always longing to kill oneself but being kept by one's watchful intelligence from killing oneself, so that the condition is stabilized in the form of lifelong controlled suffering, it's an art possessed only by this people and those belonging to it. We're a nation of suicides," writes Krankheit, "but only a small percentage actually kill themselves, even though ours is the highest percentage of suicides in the world, even though we in this country hold the world's record for suicide. What mainly goes on in this country and among these people is thinking about suicide, everywhere, in the big cities, in the towns, in the country, a basic trait of this country's population is the constant thought of suicide, they might be said to take pleasure in thinking constantly, steadily, without allowing anything to distract them, about how to do away with themselves at any time. It is their way of keeping their balance," so Krankheit's narrator, "to think constantly about killing themselves without actually killing themselves. But of course the rest of the world doesn't understand, and so whatever they think about us and regardless of what they say about us and of how they always and invariably treat us, every single one of us, they are all wrong. It's a simple fact," Krankheit writes in *Corruption,* "that our country is misunderstood, no matter how well intentioned the rest of the world may appear, what it sees when it looks at Austria and its people is total madness as a stable state of mind, a constant." And then, I am forced to add, there is the matter of the Cone, so called. It is this matter, the matter of the Cone, that occupies the central character of *Corruption,* occupies him to such a degree that one may feel justified in using the word *preoccupation,* or even *thematic preoccupation,* with respect to it, a preoccupation that is itself a central difficulty for understanding. For what is not as widely known here as it may be in some quarters, but which is nonetheless possibly of outstanding significance in this connection, is the fact Wittgenstein himself, of whose "life and philosophy" this so-called novel, so the back cover, is alleged to be a treatment, by the publishers of course, those least likely to know, nevertheless it is a fact that Wittgenstein himself did take on a building project, a most unusual enterprise in *architectural design and construction,* specifically for one of his sisters, an enterprise of vast dimensions both in its complexity of conception and its precision of execution. Nor can there be any doubt about the fact that Wittgenstein did devote several years of his life to the project of the design and construction of this remarkable edifice, for the sister to whom he was so deeply attached, just as the central character in the novel by Krankheit also devotes all his mental energies, strains his intellectual resources to the utmost, in the construction and execution of the Cone, an utterly unique and extraordinary dwelling set precisely in the centre of the Kobernausser forest, for the sister concerning whom he had the most profound feelings, and it is this, of course, which poses the *great problem,* the problem of interpretation, of understanding the meaning, if any, or the possibly symbolic meaning, if any, of this gesture. Is the building of the Cone and the central character's obsession with its perfection of conception and execution, an obsession so obsessive that he is led continually to correct, and then re-correct, and re-correct his re-corrections to the design, this most central of motifs in the story Krankheit has constructed, is this matter of the design and construction of the Cone by the novel's central character to be taken literally, or symbolically? Are we to see in the matter of the Cone a parallel to Wittgenstein's architectural endeavours alone, or, as the back cover suggests, to his philosophical endeavours alone, or are we to see it instead as a metonym for *the whole thing,* the *entire life,* of which each, the building and the philosophizing, are to be seen as facets, expressions as surprising and distinctive in their ways as can possibly be imagined but nevertheless informed by a shared impulse, an impulse to perfection, ultimately self-destructive and pursued with all the appalling energy of an obsession? But if we do this, if we go this far, which is after all only the shortest possible distance, the barest scratching of the surface in the matter of the literal or symbolic significance of Krankheit's "novelistic treatment," so called, of "the life and philosophy of Wittgenstein," so alleged, if we do even this much, then we are forced *immediately and irrevocably* to reflect on the similarity between *this* central character in *this* novel by Krankheit and *other* central characters in *other* novels by Krankheit, and so, when we have just barely begun, when we have merely scratched the surface, we find ourselves having to confront the possible role or possible non-role of Wittgenstein in *all* Krankheit's novels, and are required to reflect on what this possible role or possible non-role could conceivably be. Here we enter on considerations of the greatest complexity and delicacy, whether on the one hand we are dealing with an entire œuvre, or at least an overwhelming portion of it, which must be viewed as a "novelistic treatment," or words to that effect, of "the life and philosophy of Wittgenstein," or whether the figure of Wittgenstein is being viewed by Krankheit as somehow the *embodiment of the Austrian predicament,* a predicament that Krankheit himself feels most keenly, though what exactly this predicament is becomes a matter for debate, concerning, as it then would, the suggestion that Wittgenstein's philosophy, that is, presumably, his ideas, his thought, as well as his obsessive and self-critical temperament, may be at stake, and notwithstanding Krankheit's clear assertion that the predicament is the national preoccupation with doing away with oneself. Krankheit's focus is almost exclusively on temperament, on *archetypal temperament* one is tempted to say, and everything surrounding it and how this obsessive and self-destructive approach to life, an approach utterly characteristic of Krankheit's characters, must be a matter for some concern, else why write so many novels about it? And the fact is that while there is much here, both in the central character of this particular novel by Krankheit and in the characters of all the other novels, to remind one temperamentally of Ludwig Wittgenstein, or someone very like him, his nephew for example, if he had one, depression, perfectionism and the like, plus, in this novel, a host of significant related details, details that echo or parallel the course of Ludwig Wittgenstein's international and family involvements, and Wittgenstein's father was, of course, an industrialist, but that there's a connection between perfectionism and self-destructiveness is hardly news, Freud was from Vienna too, the question must inevitably become how all these matters of temperament, in many respects entirely central to Krankheit's apparent understanding of Austrian society, *how* all these matters are to be seen in relation to Wittgenstein's undeniably remarkable views on abstract questions of truth, language, and mathematics, and the fact that he did not in fact commit suicide. Wittgenstein was not a skeptic in the Pascalian sense, although he certainly had his doubts about academic philosophy, and to construe him either as an existentialist or as a fideist is, quite simply, to make a mistake, though he likely felt the force of the existentialist response to life in the trenches, who wouldn't. The trope that reason has its limits is, of course, the mainstay of two thousand years of Christian philosophy, and has been the centrepiece of secular metaphysics, so called, since Hume, and if you deny God into the bargain, you can get to *La Nausée,* but Wittgenstein's thought is in all respects more complex. It's true he admired the certitude of Tolstoy and Augustine, their faith, one might call it, in humanity, notably absent in Pascal, which may mean that Krankheit's point is that such distinctions are too nice and *really,* whatever Wittgenstein's preference in reading matter, Pascal got it right, and Wittgenstein's life demonstrates this. Wittgenstein always held fast to the possibility of meaning, which he compared to going up to someone, a gesture of intimacy, and it may be difficult to achieve, or to understand, but then intimacy itself is rare and difficult, it requires more courage than we frequently have, and the same is true of meaning. What is simplistic about some existentialisms is the idea that if the possibility of complete systematic meaning is denied it follows that no meaning whatsoever is possible, but of course this leaves out the possibility of non-systematic meaning, only someone incapable of thinking outside systematic structures would reject the possibility from the outset, and it is precisely this possibility that Wittgenstein explores, though with what success is, of course, debatable, and maybe that is what Krankheit is debating. What makes the matter even more difficult to assess is the personality of Krankheit himself, who, like some of his characters spent a lot of time thinking about Pascal's *Pensées,* and the radical divergence of opinion concerning his work in the secondary literature, is he a crank or a consummate genius, and indeed the extent to which he appears to elude the critical grasp of his fellow Austrians, or what comes down to the same thing, how far one can trust the copy on the backs of books, maybe Krankheit did not intend *Corruption* to be *about* Wittgenstein at all. There are all the prizes and the talk of his "startling originality," he's been hailed by some as the greatest, most brilliant of recent Austrian intellectuals, an opinion that there is reason to speculate he may have held of himself, *vide* the autobiographical novels, but then there is all that stuff about vanity in Pascal and perhaps Krankheit was simply trying to illustrate the point. And on the other hand, he, Krankheit, is condemned by other critics, in the plainest terms, for producing works that are riddled with contradictions, for mounting a shallow critique of Austrian society and mores, a critique whose shallowness is at once apparent on the most cursory inspection, so Krankheit's detractors. These works, the detractors urge, these so-called novels and autobiographical novels, and there are the plays, too, these works contain a condemnation of Austrian society and mores that *cannot be taken seriously,* cannot be thought to have any meaning, owing to its existentialist premises, so called, which proclaim the impossibility that existence has any meaning whatsoever. This is only one, though undoubtedly the worst, of the contradictions with which Krankheit's texts, the novels and autobiographical novels and plays, are alleged to be full, and the objection to it is as old as skepticism itself, the whole debate is as old as the hills, if nothing has any meaning, if we are all condemned to insanity, bestiality, criminality, suicide, or, now, the degradation that will be the inevitable consequence of environmental collapse, how can Krankheit's criticisms of society for fostering these conditions have any point, if it is all genuinely meaningless then it must also be meaningless to say that it's all meaningless. But of course the problem is with the generalization, the universal and thus self-referential claim that *everything is meaningless,* and if, like Krankheit, you proceed case by case and leave the generalizations to your critics, then, as centuries of skeptics have been aware, the damning accusation can never be made to stick, or you can say the contradiction just proves your point that reason is powerless to prevent itself from degenerating into a hopeless tangle, basically it's completely useless and we're better off to admit this from the start. We are never capable, at any time, even in our most sincere moments, of meaning, thus, by implication, Krankheit. The universe is irrational and incomprehensible to human beings and, as far as we can tell, essentially bent on the production of ever more and more horrible forms of deformity and insanity, so Krankheit. The solution is not to attempt to construct systems that will, for a moment, seem to find some local bit of order in the chaos, nor to impose the invented order of social customs and mores on what is, after all, a hopelessly revolting and stultifying state of affairs, so, by implication, Krankheit, but simply to accept that there is no solution, which acceptance is itself *undoubtedly another manifestation of the sickness,* so, we might postulate, Krankheit. The seriousness of the attempt to understand anything will be fraught with moral considerations of the most pressing nature. Or, as Krankheit writes in *Grotesqueries,* "To us every object is one that has the form of the world, that leads back to the world's history, no matter what object. Even the concepts that enable us to understand it have the form of the world for us, both the inner and the outer form of the world. We have not yet overcome the world in our thinking. But we make more progress in our thinking when it leaves the world utterly behind. At any moment we must be prepared to jettison all concepts." So Krankheit; or so, in the first three sentences, Kant, or Wittgenstein. And what then are we to set store by, the meaninglessness, and so the frivolity, of all utterance, including frivolous utterance, or the attempt to wrest meaning from meaninglessness? Does any such attempt itself render the meaninglessness meaningful, or does it simply confirm its oppressiveness, its way of simply making one appear stupid as well as revolting? Krankheit himself. And what are we to make of the last page of this novel, its poetic compression, its outright contradiction of previous statements, the final sentence, its gesture towards deep imagistic connectedness, as though ultimately everything were deliberate, every word worked over with the most extreme deliberation. The attempt any writing would represent. We are capable at each moment of the greatest intensity of meaning. Every phrase, every syllable, at each point, of the greatest meaning, the most profound content. The blank page. The eternal silence of those infinite spaces.

Being Will Be Here, Beauty Will Be Here, But This Beauty That Visits Us Now Will Be Gone

Weather. When I was a kid on the farm in Alberta, everything depended on it: what you put on in the morning and what you ate for breakfast; what you did at any given hour of the day and with whom you did it; my grandfather's, my mother's, and my own mood. And we talked about it constantly — "Did you notice? Clouding over in the west," "If it clears off now, she'll freeze," "It's already over 70° [in those days we still used Fahrenheit], gonna be a scorcher" — the hourly, sometimes minute-by-minute, warp on which our lives were strung. Much later in my life, I had a job that often had me on the road late at night between Saint John and Fredericton. To keep myself awake, I listened to the radio. My favourite part was always the late-night marine forecast: although I'd never been in a fishing boat in my life, nor seen the straits, banks, and fans the reports named, there, alone in the dark on a New Brunswick highway, I felt profoundly at home — connected, through the significance of weather, to a life like my own.

≈

Before the move to the Maritimes, I'd spent several years in Southwestern Ontario, a region renowned for its muggy summer heat and slow-witted thunderstorms. One July afternoon in 1988, I was hanging out a load of laundry. It had been hot for days, the temperature parked in the thirties, but around noon a breeze had sprung up and I figured we were in for a change. It was, in fact, downright windy by the time I got the clothes to the line — but, to my surprise, there wasn't a cloud in sight. There was a haze on the horizon, but I realized it was dust. As I pegged, the shirts and towels jerking from my hands in the wind, I was overcome with unease. It was hot, it was incredibly hot. I paused, and looked again for clouds on the horizon. Nothing. And then it struck me: the wind *itself* was hot. It was actually making things hotter. I touched the clothes I'd hung out first — already dry. And the phrase entered my mind: "It's *too* hot." I didn't know exactly what I meant by "too," except that the hair on the back of my neck was rising. This wind was like none I had experienced. It didn't belong. By the time I got back into the house, I was shaking.

Of course — I told myself that evening — one hot day does not a global catastrophe make. What I'd experienced that afternoon was at the upper end of the range for Ontario, yes, but not completely outside it. It was proof of nothing. Still: there had been something about the character of that wind: its dryness, its persistence, the absence of clouds, the way it had come, by itself, out of the southeast. I still can't find the words to capture exactly what struck me as wrong. But I can say that the problem wasn't just the temperature; it was some complex cumulative effect at the peripheries of awareness, the touch of something weird.

I've caught the same faint whiff of horror a number of times in the last couple of decades. One time, my mother rang from the farm in Alberta. "Remember I said I was moving the outhouse? Herb was in to dig the hole today." Pause. "It was dry six feet down. Like dust." That's all she said. I couldn't think of anything to say either. She knew I knew that my grandfather had insisted they'd made it through the drought in the '30s because there was always a touch of moisture, from somewhere, in the osmotic lacustrine clays that underlay the gumbo he farmed. A summer later, I sat in the porch of the new house, watching the topsoil from the garden lift and blossom in the wind like smoke. I'd read *As for Me and My House*. I knew it had been as bad, or worse, in Saskatchewan. But this wasn't happening in Saskatchewan. It was happening to the north and west, on what was supposed to be the cold damp boreal fringe of the Great Plains, not its dry, sunny heart. Sitting there, watching the soil billow and drift, I felt a sick grief. I'd have done almost anything to make it stop; and there was nothing I could do.

More recently, in the summer of 2021, on the island off the west coast where I now live, there was a so-called heat dome: a gigantic pool of hot air, lifted by convection from the western Pacific — where La Niña had built up heat in the ocean — and trapped under a cap of intense high pressure. For weeks after it passed, I surfaced from sleep into panic. It wasn't just memories of the deer, pain in her eyes, trying to crawl under the deck, or the hairy woodpecker, lying on the railing, its beak wide open, panting. It was ongoing manifestations of the land's trauma. Plants that appeared to have survived the heat dome itself were, weeks later, keeling over, one day to the next. Cedars, blueberries, raspberries, salal with western exposures looked like someone had passed a blowtorch over them. The tomatoes in the greenhouse developed tiny pale-edged holes in their leaves, as though they were being attacked by flea beetles, only there were no flea beetles. Ranks of corn turned white overnight. Salmonberries dropped all their leaves. Again, it was a sense of helplessness that drove the panic, combined with terror. The heat was destructive, but even more disturbing was the light. It had extraordinary intensity; it manifested as *radiation*. And that's what the plants were dying of: radiation sickness.

Meanwhile, work went ahead on TMX, on the Coastal GasLink export pipeline, on Site C, whose main purpose is to power tar sands extraction. LNG development permits continued to be approved.

~

But let's return to my earlier observation that one hot day in Southwestern Ontario is not tantamount to proof that global warming is occurring. The same is true of dry spells on the Prairies: it's always been touch-and-go there. The archaeological record suggests that the region was subject to prolonged and severe drought during the Hypsithermal — the peak of the warming trend that followed the Wisconsin glaciation. And come to that, isn't the current interglacial supposed to be coming to an end? In certain regions — like the Palliser triangle — it looks like the 'anomalous' weather was the wet stuff that suggested to John Macoun in 1879 that European-style agricultural settlement could be sustained there, not the dry stuff that's since made it difficult. The heat dome was reported in the media as a "one-in-a-thousand-years" event: that is, possible (though, it was granted, unlikely) without human-induced warming. Observations of this sort have been used for decades to pooh-pooh anxiety about anthropogenic climate catastrophe, and they are not without warrant. A person might be upset about bad times down on the farm, but intuitive alarm bells over single weather events are not grounds for thinking the climate *as a whole* is changing. They are, after all, merely intuitions whose focus is single events. They're not statistical science.

What does science say about climate change and the sorts of worries I've been having? Here's an analogy. Think of the way a pointillist painting works. At a distance of ten feet, even six, it all makes sense: we can see the tree, the sailboat, the river — the larger shapes and patterns that determine the meaning of the painting. But now imagine you are an ant crawling on the painting's surface. You find yourself on a splotch of beige. Does this mean you are on the pavements of the promenade? Or perhaps the walls of the clock tower? By no means. You could be on a highlight on some passer-by's black hat. No single dab of colour is impossible anywhere; and sometimes the overall effect is the result of a surprising series of local juxtapositions. Individual dots of colour have surprisingly little to do with what we perceive when we stand back. What science tells us is that weather is to climate as the dots are to the big picture.

The main consequence of the analogy is that the ant is not justified in drawing conclusions about the painting from any given splotch on which it finds itself. Even if it finds itself in an area with a lot of beige dots, it might be on a bit of cloud showing through the branches of a tree, or a patch of sunlight reflecting off the water. If it's a very big painting — and climate is: a *very* big painting — it may take generations of ants, and pooled data from ants in other regions, to begin to firm up one's hunch. Climate, although its foundation is the weather that surrounds our daily lives, is actually something quite abstract — a collection of aggregated averages that have no concrete instantiation. Climate is like the 2.3 children possessed by the average Canadian family; weather is the actual kids — integers only, we hope — fooling around in the backyard. The importance of not viewing weather events as confirmation of climate change has been heavily emphasized by bodies like the IPCC, which seeks a consensus of all its members, including the most conservative, before making public pronouncements.

But a second consequence of the analogy is also worth drawing out, if only because we may lose sight of it in insisting on the first. It's not as if there's *no* connection between climate and individual weather events. If the ant finds itself in an area with a lot of beige dots, and then suddenly crosses into an area with mostly blue ones, it would be reasonable for it to speculate that it had crossed a boundary of some sort and had entered a different region of the painting, even if that difference is merely the difference between water with sunlight glare and water without. That is, although the connection between climate and local weather is not immediate, it's there. Just as the ants never experience the big picture, we never directly perceive climate. But our experience of weather, especially over the long term and in connection with other things like native vegetation, is nonetheless relevant to our sense of what the larger pattern might be.

Moreover, despite trends in the style of Western European thinking over the last five hundred years, we remain a species that tends to make sense of immediate experience by picking up on patterns that inform it. We share this tendency, I believe, with every other species on the planet, and, although our interest in developing our capacities for systematic reconstruction has blunted our trust in gestalt perception, the ability to pick up on big pictures (or changes in big pictures) from 'mere details' remains part of our genetic inheritance. In terms of the analogy: so we're plodding merrily along, first a beige splotch, then a blue one, then a beige, then a blue, ah yes, we're out on the river amid ripples scintillating in sunlight, then a red one, then a beige, then a what? red?... hmmm — then a blue, then another red, I guess it must be sunset... Wait a minute. What if I'm off course? Aren't those blue-&-beige alterations a bit too *regular* for ripples? Uh-oh: that red's not red, it's rust! I'm on the *tent awning* way on the other side of the river and those blotches of colour are *birds*.

Carlo Ginzburg, in a discussion of scientific method, has linked a capacity for accurate medical diagnosis to 'detective' ability and to connoisseurship — that is, to a general sensitivity to the 'telling' detail. The existence of a genuine capacity of this sort need not, in terms of our analogy, be taken as licensing snake oil salespersons. Sometimes the fine diagnostician does know exactly what's wrong, and also knows, or senses, exactly what's required. But often enough, what they pick up is simply that something's not right, that more research is required. An awareness that something isn't right can be the goad to the labour of detailed empirical investigation that otherwise might not be deemed necessary.

Is intuition of this sort infallible? Of course not. Is its fallibility a reason never to pay attention to what it's suggesting? No. Intuition told me it was "too" hot that July afternoon in Southwestern Ontario, it told me it was "too" dry on the farm, and it told me that the heat dome was a foretaste of the future. My attentiveness to weather, always high, has been heightened. I'm scanning the horizon. I'm listening, intently, to what the other-than-human inhabitants of the place are telling me.

≈

To be told that human-induced global warming is a reality is the cultural equivalent of being diagnosed with a life-threatening disease. In this case, ill-health has been precipitated by an addiction; and, as is frequently the case with many addicted human individuals, the cultural damage has spread well beyond the limits of the addictee's own physical precincts.

We were told in the '60s that the Western (and, increasingly, Eastern) European lifestyle was not conducive to good health. A number of recent articles have documented the successful efforts of the fossil fuel industry to derail concerted government action. We've also been told that by the time symptoms of climate cataclysm become obvious, it will be too late to reverse them: there's a time lag between emissions and effects. The Precautionary Principle, which surfaced in discussions of environmental degradation as early as the '70s, was enshrined as Principle 15 of the Rio Declaration on Environment and Development in 1992. When I woke up to the environmental crisis in 1976, David Suzuki was saying that we had until the early '90s to turn things around. I got to work in various ways, but by the mid-'90s emissions were still rising. There was a dip in 2019 and 2020 owing to pandemic lockdowns, but emissions are on the rise again. And now the symptoms are everywhere.

Denial, as we all know, is a common phenomenon. As Alcoholics Anonymous and other twelve-step programs acknowledge, overcoming it is crucial to overcoming addiction: "Hi, my name is _____, and I'm addicted to a style of life sustained by resource extraction." Try saying it. Try counting the ways. Be sure to include your banking arrangements, your use of cash and credit and debit, all of which depend on a financial system deeply enmeshed with the continued development of oil and gas. Include, too, all non-local refrigerated items at the grocery store — orange juice and soymilk, for example — as well as jet travel (for any reason), living where you can't bike or walk to work, plastic, Gore-Tex™, polar fleece, anything made of steel, the concrete in your porch steps.... Denial often masquerades as hope, which our culture views as virtuous. And it may be manifest both before and after diagnosis. Before diagnosis, it consists in a refusal to go to the doctor to find out if anything is wrong: *especially* if we've been heavy smokers for years, we may be unable to take the persistent cough and shortness of breath seriously. It *has* to be a stubborn cold (a 'blip' in the weather pattern). After diagnosis, denial can take the form of a rejection of test results — "Everybody knows you get a lot of false positives, eh?" — or a downplaying of the seriousness of the consequences — "Hey, they can cure anything these days" (we'll just spray megatonnes of calcium carbonate into the stratosphere).

∼

Global warming is only one of several human-induced environmental cataclysms. Robert Bringhurst puts the point succinctly:

Being will be here.
Beauty will be here.

But this beauty that visits us now will be gone.

It is hubris to imagine our species can destroy everything, or even everything that matters to it, just as it is hubris to imagine we are what evolution is 'for,' or that human interests are distinct from and ontologically superior to those of other beings.

"Why is there something rather than nothing?" — A question that has no answer, but one that is rooted in a fact that has absorbed and moved great thinkers from Lǎo Zi to Martin Heidegger. Which is not to say that you have to be a philosophical genius to experience astonishment that things *exist*: it's a common experience among the naturalists and poets of my acquaintance. And I'll bet dollars to doughnuts many of the folks leaning in, listening to those late-night marine forecasts, felt it from time to time. Our astonishment is the mark of our mortality. Is-ness *is,* always; but *what* is, *this,* is here only now. The love we feel for tangible particulars — a stand of birch, a stretch of river, no less than other human beings — is as biologically basic as our sexual mode of reproduction. We must love what dies and we must love *because* we die. Plato, like other religious thinkers in other traditions, sought to ease the pain attendant on this inheritance by encouraging us to fix our erotic gaze on eternity, on the non-particularized being that informs everything that is. But me, I'm with Herakleitos: "The things of which there is seeing, hearing, and perception, these do I prefer." I would be the last to deny the power of universal, atemporal being; it's just that because I'm human — that is, because I love and die — it's only half the story. "Nameless:" says the *Dào Dé Jīng,* "the origin of heaven and earth. / Naming: the mother of ten thousand things." Those ten thousand things are the other half of the story. They are the manifestations through which the mystery flows, without which it would be invisible, of which each of us is one.

A mere twenty years ago, it made sense to believe that immediate, aggressive global actions might forestall the worst consequences of human-induced climate change. But those actions were not taken. It is my belief that there is no action now, none, that will reverse the major ecosystem collapses that are underway. This summer, we lost a dozen trees, as well as salal, saskatoons and moss, on the west-facing slope south of the house. The moss may reassert itself if we have a few cool summers, but there will not be time for the larger plants to regenerate before the next heat dome. In a few decades the weather will, as a matter of course, be too hot and too dry here for sword ferns, deer ferns, hemlock, spruce, salmonberries, alders, coast Douglas-fir, red cedars, grand firs, balsam firs, Pacific maples, dogwoods, and shore pine, and many of the mammals, insects, amphibians, birds, and molluscs that live among them. This beauty will be gone.

And there is now no hope, none, in any consequentialist sense of that word, that things might turn out allright. As Warren Heiti has written, "Anyone who has ever been arrested by [the radiant beauty of beings] knows that what humans are doing is unspeakable. The strain of trying to comprehend it shatters the imagination." There is hope in this sense only: that some among us, as individuals, might own what we have done, might feel a grief appropriate to the size, complexity, intricacy, and generosity of what we are destroying, and a horror equal to the savagery with which that destruction has been pursued. In this way, some among us, as individuals, may find ourselves fully present to the beauty that is here now.

But whether or not we do, the tide of being will wash over us, and we will be gone.

A Note on Jane Jacobs's *Systems of Survival*, or Why We Will Not Be Able to Prevent Global Ecological Collapse

At key points in the *Republic*, Plato's great dialogue about how to remedy injustice in the individual soul and in the state at large, we find reference to seeking 'to outdo others.' To want to outdo others is to be governed by *pleonexia*, a desire for more and more, a desire for more than enough. Pleonexia, Plato argues, is the root of injustice; it leads to wanting what isn't yours. To be just, by contrast, is to want and to do only, and exactly, what is your own. Justice can be achieved, Plato suggests, through the coordinated exercise of three other virtues: self-restraint, courage, and wisdom. He intended the *Republic* not just as a portrait of the ideal state and individual, but also as a critique of existing attitudes and methods of government. It failed to save the day. By the time Plato wrote it, the brutal and bloated Athenian empire was sliding irretrievably into chaos. The American empire — another brutal and pleonectic culture — is also collapsing, and the disintegration of a 'progressive' world order is taking place amid the biospheric catastrophe that it has spawned. It is too late, as it was too late in Plato's Athens, to urge the virtues of self-restraint and wisdom on the state. We are left to attempt meaningful moral gestures as individuals and small communities rather than as voting members of large national polities.

The virtue now most required by those of us who enjoy the supermarkets, the drinkable tap water, and the air-conditioning offered by Western so-called liberal democracies is courage: courage to admit our individual complicity in ecological catastrophe and courage to admit that we belong to a remarkably violent, intemperate, and short-sighted species. These acts of self-recognition may, in turn, give us the integrity to die well.

Are there special 'ecological' virtues that we ought to have practised? No. If we look at stories from surviving pre-colonial cultures, we see that there is significant overlap between the virtues they praise and the virtues praised by pre-Christian European cultures. (Indeed, there is even some overlap among the virtues admired in pre-colonial cultures and those advocated by monotheistic religions.) The core set is the same as Plato's: courage, self-restraint, sagacity or wisdom, and fair dealing — that is, justice. That these four canonical virtues have been repeatedly urged on us for millennia suggests that humans as a species are prone to greed, to cheating, to rash and stupid behaviour, and to refusing to face up to these facts about themselves. Stories promoting the canonical virtues, bolstered by warnings about the consequences of failing to observe them, are meant to make communal life possible, and to help humans live equitably, not only with each other but with the rest of the world's inhabitants — on whose well-being their own well-being depends.

However, all cultures also attest to a list of shadow virtues: trickery and thievery; impulsive bravado; clever deceit; ham-fisted violence in males, as long as it's powerful enough to suppress opposition; and vanity in females, as long as it secures them a mate. We see pleonexia operating in one form or another in all of them. I call them *virtues* because they are traits that are admired and cultivated; indeed, they are regarded as forms of human excellence. I call them *shadow* virtues because, although this admiration is real, it is covert. The shadow virtues are rarely explicitly acknowledged as admirable: thievery isn't thievery if everyone agrees to it; deceit isn't deceit unless its practitioner pretends honesty; vanity that parades itself openly is usually regarded as pitiable or disgusting. Where admiration is explicit, these shadow virtues are consolidated in trickster figures and in stories of male aggression in war.

It is the triumph of the shadow virtues, sustained and promoted by advertising (itself often a form of clever deceit), that has led to global environmental catastrophe. The old stories have always warned us of the consequences of succumbing to shadow ideals; and they have always told us that it's in our nature to think we can get away with flouting the canonical virtues until it's too late.

Whence these shadow virtues? Why are they so resistant to control by the canonical virtues? How is it that, intelligent though we are, they are proving our — and many other species' — undoing?

In *Systems of Survival,* Jane Jacobs describes two distinct constellations of human virtues that show up pan-culturally, at least in urbanized cultures. So-called traders condemn violence and value cooperation, transparency, and social equality; so-called guardians condemn trading, and value the hierarchical organization of power, displays of prowess, secrecy, and an us-*versus*-them approach to the world. Examples of guardian institutions in the West include the Mafia, the NSA, CSIS, the military, some religious orders, industrial monopolies, the police, aristocracies, and government bureaucracies; they used to include symphony orchestras and the academy. Traders 'institutionalize' less often; the style is epitomized in the person running a small, innovative business or volunteer collectives seeking to better their communities.

Here are Jacobs's lists of the characteristics associated with each moral paradigm:

THE TRADER MORAL SYNDROME	THE GUARDIAN MORAL SYNDROME
shun force	*shun trading*
come to voluntary agreements	*exert prowess*
be honest	*be obedient and disciplined*
collaborate easily with strangers	*be exclusive*
compete	*respect hierarchy*
respect contracts	*take vengeance*
use initiative and enterprise	*be loyal*
be open to inventiveness and novelty	*adhere to tradition*
be efficient	*make rich use of leisure*
promote comfort and convenience	*show fortitude*
dissent for the sake of the task	*deceive for the sake of the task*
invest for productive purposes	*treasure honour*
be industrious	*dispense largesse*
be thrifty	*be ostentatious*
be optimistic	*be fatalistic*

Jacobs discovered the two moral constellations as she puzzled over intractable problems facing North American society: the expansion of bureaucracies that waste everyone's time; the growth of ethnic tensions; the subversion of public interest by corporate greed; the persistence of vast nuclear arsenals. She decided to research the morality governing "practical working life" to see if she could figure out why these problems resisted solution. Her reading was extensive and wide-ranging. It included biographies, business histories, reports of scandals, sociology, history, and cultural anthropology. Both syndromes, Jacobs claims, share a number of 'universal' virtues, which she lists separately: courage, moderation, wisdom, common sense, competence, cooperation, foresight, judgement, perseverance, faith, energy, patience, and mercy.

Three of the four canonical virtues — moderation (self-restraint), courage, and wisdom — appear explicitly in this list. But I think they appear there under other names as well. That is, I think the list can be condensed. Perseverance, patience, and energy are specific forms of courage, inflected in the cases of perseverance and patience by self-restraint; faith, too, is a form of self-restraint — the refusal to succumb to despair; common sense, foresight, judgement, and competence are all forms of sagacity or wisdom. This leaves cooperation and mercy unaccounted for — as allegedly universal virtues over and above the canonical four. But I am not convinced that either is, in fact, universally regarded as a virtue. Cooperation is the *paradigmatic* trader virtue and is frequently dismissed as irrelevant by those who subscribe to a guardian ethos. Think of the stories that involve rogue cops or cowboys fighting for justice on their own terms, no part of a community, never working with others. And mercy appears to be a virtue associated with monotheistic religions: a curb on patriarchal rage. This is what distinguishes it from compassion, its trader complement — mercy is exercised in contexts in which there is a judicially determined right to behave cruelly. Trader communities rarely recognize such a right. In guardian cultures, mercy is frequently dispensed opportunistically, to cement loyalty in the one to whom mercy is shown. I propose, then, that we add cooperation to the list of specifically trader virtues and mercy to the list of specifically guardian virtues.

The other outstanding discrepancy between Jacobs's list of universal virtues and the standard four is the absence of justice from Jacobs's list. Consider, though, those lists of non-universal virtues, the ones that distinguish Jacobs's two paradigms. It seems to me that in several cases, what we see are the 'universal' virtues — including justice — refracted through two distinct lenses: justice *as* respect for contracts and justice *as* vengeance; self-control *as* thrift or efficiency and self-control *as* obedience; wisdom *as* honesty and openness to innovation, and wisdom *as* adherence to tradition; courage *as* willingness to collaborate and to dissent, and courage *as* prowess and fatalistic fortitude. What determines the guise in which a 'universal' virtue will appear? It looks like what we might at first be tempted to call 'moral frameworks' are, in fact, ecologies of sorts — organizations in which the parts inflect one another. Within a given moral ecology, so-called universal virtues may appear as themselves, but they may also take on inflections determined by their interactions within the whole. In their inflected versions, if Jacobs is correct, they are complemented and reinforced by other distinct virtues.

One striking feature of the lists is the degree of conflict they suggest. It is indeed little wonder that situations in which both paradigms are operating are beset by insoluble problems. Another striking feature is the presence of several shadow virtues — trickery, deceit, violence — on the guardian list.

It is even more striking, however, that pleonexia shows up — under more than one name — on both lists. In guardian mode, we *admire* ostentation and displays of largesse; we *admire* those who lie their way into power or profit and who hang onto it with an iron fist. On the other hand, if we're in a trader frame of mind, we're happy to promote excess in the guise of comfort and convenience — the marketing and consumption of useless gadgetry and of novelty for novelty's sake. "Shopping," as it used to say on the doors of The Bay in Victoria, BC, "is good." How is conspicuous consumption to be reconciled with the trader virtue of thrift? Perhaps it isn't. Perhaps we are witnessing the erosion of the trader moral code under the relentless metastasis of capitalism. But note that marketers still appeal to thrift in an effort to encourage overconsumption: everything everywhere is declared to be ON SALE! at ROCK BOTTOM PRICES! And we succumb, occasionally experiencing subsequent bewilderment at the useless stuff crowding our cupboards. Then there's capitalism itself: the unrestrained exploitation of natural 'resources' that undergirds the shibboleth of economic growth: pleonexia in the form of so-called productive investment.

When I look at the lists further, I notice something else. Although I'm willing to believe that the syndromes are exhibited pan-culturally in contemporary urbanized societies, it seems they may not have been present (and may not be present now) in all societies everywhere. They may, for instance, have been absent in at least some native North American societies at the time of European contact. I'm thinking, for example, of the Haudenosaunee and Algonquian societies described in the seventeenth-century *Relations des Jésuites de la Nouvelle-France.* In those societies, collaboration with strangers, cooperation, and optimism appear to have co-existed comfortably with exertion of prowess, the treasuring of honour, respect for tradition, and loyalty. Does such a merging of the two lists represent a third sort of moral culture? Or a collapse of distinct syndromes under certain economic and territorial conditions? Does it show that where pleonexia is made impossible by scarcity of resources, the two moral codes do not diverge? I do not know. But I think it would be worth trying to find out.

Why do we collectively fail to enact the canonical virtues in their canonical forms, even when our lives or the lives of our children depend on it? What Jacobs's syndromes suggest is that the answer arises from conflict between and within our practical moral codes.

In the first instance, change on the scale required would mean a sudden wholesale shift to a predominantly trader ethos: honesty from those in corporate and political power; massive cooperation both locally and internationally; collaboration with strangers; thrift of a profound character — which would mean openness to radical changes in lifestyle for those in rich countries. The guardians among us experience demands for this kind of behaviour as intuitively *wrong*. We can't expect them cheerfully to substitute thrift for ostentatious display; we can't expect those who occupy positions of corporate and political power — and there are many, for power, maintained by backroom deals and loyal cabals, is the guardian's native turf — suddenly to own up to the actual state of the resource base.

The second source of disabling conflict lies *within* the trader ethos itself. Pleonexia shows up not just in the form of ostentatious guardian largesse, but also in the form of trader-driven consumerism. Really to encourage the necessary thrift would require restraint on investment, an overturning of the ideal of endless economic 'growth,' and an overhaul of wealthy notions of comfort, convenience, and the pursuit of novelty. In addition, those of us who've been living beyond our ecological means would need to cultivate guardian-style fortitude in the face of an end to luxury. We'd also need a good dose of fatalism to balance the compulsory optimism that imagines there's a high-tech solution just around the corner. But part of what is entailed by the fact that the syndromes are *ecologies* is that we can't just cookie-cut the specific virtues we need. To modify any given aspect is to modify all.

How deep do the tensions go? If it weren't for the pre-colonial record, I would suspect they were biological. And we must remember that even pre-colonial cultures were rich in stories whose moral is the need for self-restraint. The pleonectic shadow virtues appear to be idealizations of desire. And why not? Desire goes very deep in the history of this planet: it is arguably part of the definition of life. If this is so, then humans turn out to be a moderately disastrous and ultimately self-cancelling evolutionary experiment — a form of life, a version of wanting, that got too good at getting.

On Rules and Moral Beauty

For obvious reasons, juntas, dictatorships, and liberal democracies figure frequently in discussions of civil liberties. Bureaucracies show up less often. This is so partly because the harms bureaucracies inflict are not usually life-threatening. People are sometimes unjustly fined, taxed, or even imprisoned by bureaucracies, but they are rarely executed or subjected to physical torture. Apart from fines and penalties, the injustices inflicted by bureaucracies tend to be spiritual rather than material. Neither the UN Declaration of Human Rights nor the Canadian Charter enshrines a right to freedom from mindless hassle. And in bureaucracies *per se,* unlike dictatorships, there is no obvious person or group of people who might benefit if liberties are abused. As Kafka understood, what is horrific about large bureaucracies is precisely their facelessness. There is no one to hold to account, no animus to confront or overthrow, and often no court of appeal. As Dickens, some sixty years earlier, had pointed out, a bureaucracy *is* sometimes all that is left of a court of appeal.

But there is a deeper reason that bureaucracies don't figure in discussions of civil liberties, and it has to do with the relationship between rules and our ability to uphold the freedoms we prize. Bureaucracies are, often enough, outgrowths of liberal democracies or other institutions with interests in equality: regulations, and the apparatus that maintains them, are among the means that democracies use to ensure fair access and fair distribution. Rules, in the form of laws, are above all the foundation of due process. As the BC Civil Liberties Association has said, the law is the "defender and enhancer" of democratic freedoms. It *protects* liberty. I agree, and would not myself want to live in a rule-less society. I am deeply grateful for rules of many sorts: they have made and continue to make my life better, from those governing the flow of traffic on city streets to those that insist I should be paid no less than my male colleagues for work of equal value. Where the rules are well made and the principles they uphold are sound, rule-following is emblematic of the conception of justice as fairness.

And yet I believe there remains a question about the relation of rules to the good life. I have in mind not only nightmarish scenarios in which people are genuinely oppressed by unintelligible bureaucratic requirements or made miserable by pressure to conform to some cultural variant of the straight and narrow. The question I want to ask can be provoked by much less insidious circumstances. Indeed, it was provoked in my own life by a sequence of very minor events. But it was, in a way, the insignificance of the episode that brought home to me the significance of the issue. For the effect was profound, and I have continued to puzzle over it.

The encounter took place in that most innocuous of locations, the circulation desk of one of our major university libraries. I had a book in hand and was hoping to be able to take it home to Quadra Island for a week. But it was not my own university library and I had forgotten my COPPUL card — a small piece of grey paper that confirmed my registration in the Council of Prairie and Pacific University Libraries Reciprocal Loan Program. The book was an old book on an obscure subject; I had my bar-coded photo-graced UVic faculty library card with me; I was hoping for, but not expecting, a break.

Sure enough, I didn't get one. Although other librarians in other situations had scarcely glanced at my COPPUL card, asking immediately for my UVic card as though demanding the real goods, the rule is: you gotta have a COPPUL card before they can ask for your library card, and I didn't have mine with me. I was in the process of putting my UVic card back in my wallet when a voice said, "I'll take it out for you." I looked up. The voice belonged to a woman who'd come up to the desk from the direction of the reserve room during my exchange with the librarian. She was around thirty, worn jacket, worn backpack, round, pleasant features. The librarian visibly stiffened. "We strongly discourage patrons from doing that." "That's okay," the woman said. She looked directly at me. "Do you need the book?" "Well, yes," I stumbled, "um, it would help a lot." "Well, then," she smiled at the librarian, "that's easy." She took out her card and put it on the book, which she pushed toward the librarian. The librarian was both flummoxed and annoyed. "Really. We recommend strongly against this." "I'd like the book," the woman said. After a short silence, the librarian swiped her card, scanned the book's bar code, and handed her the book. She, in turn, handed it to me. I thanked her, profusely, in some astonishment, and asked if I could give her my email address, or if she'd like my phone number. "No," she said, having reshouldered her backpack, already heading toward the main doors, "it's fine."

And she was right. It *was* fine. Her gesture had made it so. This was partly because of the apparent absence of an ulterior motive: she wasn't getting off on confronting the librarian, she wasn't trying to make friends with me, there were no signs of self-congratulatory halo-polishing. What had happened was this: A stranger had looked me in the eye, trusted that I needed the book and trusted that I would return it. I felt, both in the instant and on reflection, liberated.

Why?

I had not supposed I had a 'right' to the book. I would not have suffered grievous harm if, as I'd expected, I'd been denied the privilege of taking it home. The reason COPPUL cards are required — when apparently it's one's library card that really matters — eludes me, but I can imagine that such a reason might exist. (Perhaps the COPPUL card confirms that you don't have an atrocious record of not returning books to your home library.) My sense of release, of joy, had its root, I think, in the fact that I had assumed and had myself accepted that I would be reduced to the description "does not have her COPPUL card." It was liberating to be seen for what I was: a polite, if somewhat shabbily dressed, middle-aged woman with a UVic faculty card — likely a scholar and as good a risk as any to return a library book.

But no, there's something else: even more crucial was my benefactor's willingness to make herself vulnerable to my potential untrustworthiness. Her willingness to take that risk opened a space in which it was possible for me to act honourably. It made it possible for me to *be* honourable, to be the trustworthy person which, in fact, I am. This trustworthy person — who respects and loves the institution of the public lending library — this person, her honour and her love, *cannot be countenanced* by the system of rules that safeguards all of us against the greed, competitiveness, absent-mindedness, and laziness of a few. I'm very glad the collection is there when I want to use it; I support the rules that keep it functional; and yet those very rules mean that it is impossible to express, in my actions, the love and honour I actually feel. In trusting me, my benefactor made it possible for me to respond to the claim of moral beauty, and my response was alacritous.

And then there was my admiration for her courage. Experiencing courage in others tends to inspire our own — so, again, there was what we might describe as a liberation of the potential for virtue, an unfettering of my capacity to love the good. In what, precisely, did her courage consist? Since she was not actually breaking any rule, the system was not going to come after her. It consisted partly in her standing up to the disapproval of the librarian. But the librarian's nominal authority derived from the fact that she was the representative of the rules — and the larger part of my benefactor's courage lay in her standing up to the fact of the rules themselves.

For often what humans want to do is not the right thing, nor what is obviously practical, nor even what will satisfy our own interest. We're social animals. Often what we want to do is to hang with the group: we want to do what everyone else does. This compulsion to comply, which we share with many other mammals, is one source of the power of bureaucracies. It can create real anxiety around the image of resistance. It can even disguise from us the fact that certain rules, or certain rules in certain circumstances, have no point: we obey anyway, without thinking, and our obedience alone seems to be sufficient justification for the rule.

However, as I've tried to underline, not all rules *are* pointless. And in some cases, our respect for them is itself ennobling. (The most famous example might be Sokrates' decision to abjure escape and to drink the hemlock.) What, then, is the lesson here? Perhaps this: that trust makes possible a particular kind of community, a community of our best selves — selves that we sense are deeply authentic. It is as though trust is the endoskeleton that allows community to stand up and really *be* community, whereas a system of rules is an exoskeleton that straightlaces a morass of reprobates into the *shape* of a community.

But this, surely, is too simplistic. We are a species many of whose members are not, in fact, entirely trustworthy — but our communities are not thereby rendered less than real, or less worthy. A tendency to mislay library books is, as often as not, a reflection of something *else* we treasure deeply: creativity, or generosity, or flexibility, a carefree liveliness. So perhaps the lesson is more like this: We need rules, and our upholding of them can be a source of moral beauty. But we need also to perceive when trust is warranted, and when it should trump obedience.

The problem is therefore difficult. Rules for when we should obey other rules are not the answer — not only because there's a theoretical regress. A correct judgement that trust is warranted, that a given rule should in a given situation be bent or circumvented, is wholly and deeply context-dependent. The capacity for such judgement — like expertise in medical diagnosis or musical phrasing — can be learned; but it cannot be captured by rules — for, to *be* a rule, a prescription must reduce individual situations to types. What the liberation made possible by trust requires, then, is not only courage. It requires the case-by-case exercise of discernment — a capacity for non-criterialized insight into a field of circumstances, a sensitivity to the larger weather of an event.

Big bureaucracies, history suggests, are outgrowths of empire. Indeed, bureaucracy appears to be the form of government into which empires most frequently evolve as they disintegrate. It is also one of the means by which we continue the domestication of ourselves as a species. And as we populate our way over the brink of the planet's carrying capacity, we should expect regulations to proliferate. Management by rules is one of the surest ways to avoid having to respond, case by case, to the impossibly large numbers of individuals that now make up cohorts of students, ranks of employees, and the citizenry. But my unknown benefactor has set me an example. She has inspired me to hope that I will learn to distinguish wisely between situations in which the rules do need to be upheld and those in which trust, exceeding the rules, might allow us to be claimed by situation-specific moral beauty. I hope too that, should I find myself in circumstances of the latter sort, I will, like my benefactor, have the courage to act.

Lyric, Narrative, Memory

*... Everything
loud with big voices, the salt of merchandises,
pile-ups of palpitating bread,
the stalls of my suburb of Argüelles with its statue
like a drained inkwell in a swirl of hake:
oil flowed into spoons,
a deep baying
of feet and hands swelled in the streets,
metres, litres, the sharp
measure of life,
                        stacked-up fish,
the texture of roofs with a cold sun in which
the weather vane falters,
the fine, frenzied ivory of potatoes,
wave on wave of tomatoes rolling down to the sea.*

*And one morning all that was burning,
one morning the bonfires
leapt out of the earth
devouring human beings —
and from then on fire,
gunpowder from then on,
and from then on blood.
Bandits with planes and Moors,
bandits with finger-rings and duchesses,
bandits with black friars spattering blessings
came through the sky to kill children
and the blood of children ran through the streets
without fuss, like children's blood....*

> *And you will ask: why doesn't his poetry*
> *speak of dreams and leaves*
> *and the great volcanoes of his native land?*
>
> *Come and see the blood in the streets.*
> *Come and see*
> *the blood in the streets.*
> *Come and see the blood*
> *in the streets!*
>
> — PABLO NERUDA,
>   from "I'm Explaining a Few Things,"
>   translated by Nathaniel Tarn

Is there any gesture humans make that is not a species of remembering? Certainly every lyric gesture is, as Patrick Friesen says, a song of longing. Longing for what? Wholeness, I think. Integrity. A coming home to the self, which must feel like remembering — *nostos,* a return — even if we have never been home before.

≈

Narrative, too, remembers. But it does not long — at least, not in the same way. Narrative's *eros* is the *eros* of sequential order, the root of syntax, which it shares with discursive argument.

≈

Sequence is the genus of narrative's *eros*. Its species is logico-temporal consequence.

≈

Before, after, meanwhile — narrative loves temporal linkage, and loves it as the basis of causal understanding — *if, so, in spite of* ...

≈

Causality is the temporal sub-species of consequence.

≈

This is not to say that all narratives follow a simple linear order. It is to say that even in its most nonlinear presentations, riddled with foreshadowing and flashback, narrative draws its breath from our experience of meaningful sequence in time.

≈

Extended narratives often involve meditation on an image of the human self. In myth-narratives, this image is often an archetype. There can be nostalgia associated with such images, too: we say that we tell and listen to such stories in an effort to understand our lives; but frequently what this amounts to is an attempt to comfort ourselves, to make sense of what we think we were, or imagine we have become.

≈

A preoccupation with thinking about and imagining the self is not something that, as beings with a capacity for language, humans can avoid. With Freud, I believe that the distinction between self and other is the phenomenological foundation of tool-use; and I also believe that language is a tool. But, at its best and most luminous, thinking about the self can reflect an attempt to live fully in the irresoluble tension between a desire for wholeness and the capacity for tool-use, whose exercise makes the experience of wholeness impossible.

≈

From lyric's perspective, the self does not exist — what exists are moments of kenotic attention and address. The tears of the saint are, I suspect, tears over the impossibility of stitching such moments together into a pattern that looks human.

≈

To try to make sense of one's life is to gather one's own and the community's memories and to attempt to produce some kind of fit, some kind of mutual accommodation. But this project is continually undone by the world, by deep, open attention to the world. No one voices this difficulty more brilliantly than Virginia Woolf in *The Waves* — Bernard's long closing soliloquy, or Rhoda's reaction to

Percival's death. Indeed, the structure of this extended prose meditation — is it a novel? — embodies that tension. The short italicized sections that carry the plot, such as it is; and the long reaches of lyric prose that attempt

> ("But how describe the world seen without a self? There are no words. Blue, red — even they distract, even they hide with thickness instead of letting the light through.")

— that attempt to present lyric consciousness.

~

And, of course, there is narrative poetry — epic, for example, or anecdotal verse. The existence of such poetry, along with the existence of prose like Woolf's, shows that the contrast between narrative and lyric cannot be understood as a contrast between prose and poetry.

~

Lyric's intuition is that the grammars of consequence — of narrative and logical argument — distort the mystery of what-is. Lyric order, unmediated by human language, is not rational, causal, or systematic. It is, rather, resonant.

~

The world's resonance is its integrity.

~

Narrative addresses us as members of the tribe: it binds us in a common *ethos*. We *use* narrative to *make* things hang together, to tame experience so that it does not overwhelm us.

~

Narrative is the genre of choice for the historical treatment of memory. *And then,* it says. *And then, and then, and then.*

Lyric's *eros,* by contrast, is the *eros* of coherence — the absence of a hierarchical distinction between essence and accident. For lyric, everything is a centre, everything a detail. We use lyric form when we need to affirm memory as wilderness, as the raw music of experience.

≈

Lyric attempts to listen — to remember — *without* constructing, without imposing a logical or temporal order on experience. *This,* it says. *This. And this. And this.*

≈

Is narrative a debased mode of comprehension, then — somehow less true to the world than lyric? No. But narrative comprehension is informed by a different order of truth than lyric. Narrative's truth mediates between our desire for integrity and the experience of self supervenient on our species' capacity for tool-use.

≈

Narrative thinking is as natural a phenomenon as tool-use. Whether in the guise of Western Apache *godíyįhgo nagoldi'é* or seventeenth-century Western European science, it is one of the ways humans render experience.

≈

Narrative selects among events for causal relevance. It distinguishes foreground and background, protagonist and walk-on, also for causal relevance. This is what allows it to express an *ethos* — a way of existing in community, including collective beliefs about what constitutes appropriate behaviour towards other beings with whom we share the planet.

≈

Lyric disbelieves in climax, in heroes, in minor characters. Narrative knows that there is a difference between centres and details, and that if you get absorbed in or distracted by the latter at the wrong moment, you could die.

≈

Lyric is indifferent to death.

≈

Any given way of conceiving causality embodies a particular way of thinking about time, and will have associated with it a particular style of narrative.

≈

Narrative *is* a construct: what an event is is determined by its place in a sequential structure — in the Western European style: origin, development, climax, dénouement. History is the practice of temporal taxonomy, a way of sorting, of finding compartments for, the welter of events and beings that we encounter.

≈

Lyric knows the world is whole, that every part of it is integrally related to every other part — and knows that we cannot be other than overwhelmed by this recognition.

≈

Lyric resists the accommodation of events to story, as it rejects the identification of clarity with logical structure. It knows the order of the world is asyntactic.

≈

Lyric, then, is the genre of choice for the astonished treatment of memory, in particular for memory of experience that falls outside the pale of communal story-telling.

≈

Lyric address to the past stands as an implied critique of the shapeliness of history: it insists on a movement from sequence to haecceity.

History, we are told, is written by the winners. As mortal beings, however, we are constantly losers of the world, and of that communion with the world for which, as creatures of language, we will always long.

≈

Many things fall outside the pale of communal story-telling. I will focus on just two: memory of atrocity and memory of grace.

≈

To *historicize* atrocity, to turn memory of it into a story, is to insist that sense can be made of it, that it can be located in a causal order, and that by so locating it, we can come to terms with it.

≈

But this is not true. What makes atrocity *atrocity* is that it is outside the reach of intelligible causal accounts. There is no sane *ethos* that can embrace it. Its memory, then, cannot be documented *morally* in narrative. Moral treatment of atrocity requires a lyric medium: witness rather than explanation.

≈

To convey an experience of grace narratively is also to provide an explanation of it. Narrative tames the mystery at the heart of grace by fitting it into a causal order: it is a reward for good behaviour, say, or an explanation of luck.

≈

But grace, like atrocity, eludes causally intelligible order. It just *is* lyric experience — a moment when the scales fall from our eyes, ears, every sense, and we know the world as a resonant whole. Characteristic of such recognition is its atemporality — the glimpse it affords that time is unreal.

≈

As concepts, narrative and lyric are distinct. As practical strategies of utterance, they are not necessarily separated on the ground. Are there mixed genres? Of course. Are there genreless works that employ both lyric and narrative structure? Of course. Is it possible to use the words "And then ... and then ... and then ..." and mean "This! ... And this! ... And this!"? Of course.

~

"Why do I remember this?" It is not the *content* of narrative's answer that is important, but the fact that it tries to answer at all. Lyric knows the answer is nothing more than, nothing less than, the resonant moment, saturated with meaning, the world's whole, its uncountable interrelated aspects, singing through it.

~

A stranger am I, was a stranger born.
A stranger even in the autumn of my life.
With old eyes I look back.

Where do we come from? What is our soul?
A mist over darkened water, the beam of a cowhouse-lantern,
of a star?

With my hand over my old eyes,
       which were once those of a child —
... the house of the dead
in the late autumn evening.
Someone enters with heavy tread
setting the cowhouse-lantern down at the door
enters into the starlight.
Now none are missing ...

Why do I remember this?

 — PÄR LAGERKVIST,
  from "With old eyes I look back,"
  translated by W.H. Auden and Leif Sjöberg

The Syntax of Ethical Style

Does poetry, as a genre, speak in a particularly significant way to issues of environmental concern? If so, how? Can it make a difference to the unfolding catastrophes that we now inhabit?

These are complex questions because there are many competing opinions about what we should do about climate cataclysm and its fallout: extinctions, crop failures, soil depletion, water shortages, droughts, floods; many competing opinions about what we should do about human overpopulation, atmospheric degradation caused by air traffic, plastic pollution, noise pollution, light pollution, invasive species, and overfishing. Are we asking how poetry can move governments to *do something*? Or how it can incite our neighbours to reduce, reuse, and recycle? Do we want poetry to fix things, or to help us learn to die? I have views about what can and ought to be done, but I know they aren't universally shared; and it's not my aim to debate facts and policies.

The question is also complex because many different things get called 'poetry': epic verse, nursery rhymes, prose poetry, strings of sentences that use only one vowel. Because of this complexity, I'm going to shift the focus away from poetry to what I've come to call lyric thought. Lyric thought is a big genus, too, but luckily it has a concise definition: it's thought driven by intuitions of radical coherence. In this definition, the 'lyre' in 'lyric' rises to prominence: lyric thought means the way music does. It is thought whose structure is resonant, in which each aspect is tuned by the whole. Examples include the paintings of Mary Pratt, the jazz improvisations of Bill Evans, and the *Tractatus Logico-Philosophicus* by Ludwig Wittgenstein. Lyric thought also includes a good deal of poetry, but the standard English Department definition of lyric poetry — poetry that is an outpouring of the individual ego — isn't on the radar here. In what I'm calling lyric thought, including lyric poetry, the human ego is present merely as a reference point for perception of the world; and sometimes that ego comes close to dissolving entirely.

The question, then, becomes: Is lyric thought, of any kind, ethically relevant in a time of ecological cataclysm? The answer, I believe, is yes: lyric thinking, because of its resonant structure, is uniquely suited to bearing witness. In developing this answer, I'll begin with a look at the traditionally close relationship between ethics and narrative in many cultures. It turns out that there are at least two distinct kinds of what I'll call narrative *syntax*, by which I mean two different ways in which narratives can be put together. Each of these types of narrative syntax conditions a distinct kind of moral thought. But there are also gestures that we instinctively recognize as moral that don't seem to fit either kind of narrative syntax. What we see in these gestures is a response to a morally problematic situation, without an attempt to recommend action. No policy, no 'fix,' is prescribed. The moral realignment that witness achieves is inner, inarticulate, and ungeneralizable.

Ethics and Narrative

To narrate, the dictionary tells us, is to relate or to recount. The word, interestingly, does not come into frequent use in English until the mid-eighteenth century, but when it arrives it does so directly from the Latin *narrāre*. If we look further, under *relate*, the dictionary repeats itself: "to recount, narrate, tell...." But the etymology here refers us to *refer*, and there things get a little more interesting. The root of *refer* is *referre*, from *re-* or again, plus *ferre*, to bear or carry. To narrate, then, is *to bear or carry something again*. The repeated presence of 'tell' and 'recount' in the lists of synonyms suggests that the something in question is a sequence. (*Tell* originally meant to count or to reckon up, as the phrase *bank teller* still indicates.) If this is correct, then narrative form must be capable of carrying sequences; it must be a sequential structure.

So much, we might say, is utterly obvious. Narratives characteristically say *first ... and then ... and then*. But we need to ask about what goes into those blanks. For narratives typically *select* among actions, events, and facts. "First the telephone rang and then a dust mote fell and then the fridge cut in and then a beetle landed on the windowsill and then the Canadian prime minister announced the approval of the Trans Mountain Pipeline extension and then Kate's mosquito bite started to itch" is not a narrative. Or, if we insist that it is, we're probably trying for some special effect: we know that we're working against default expectations. These default expectations are important. They're pan-cultural. They show us something deep about how narrative means. In standard narrative form, we expect at least some of the events that fit in the *and then ... and then...* slots to be *consequences* of what went in the *first...* slot. We expect events that *aren't* obviously consequences to be at the head of some other *and then... and then...* chain. In other words, in standard narrative form at least some members of the sequence *follow from* other members of the sequence.

Let's pause a moment and ask what we mean by 'follow from' here. There are at least two kinds of consequence. "My bum knee is a result of overuse" is an example of *causal* consequence, while "Sokrates is mortal because he is human and all humans are mortal" is an example of *logical* consequence. And, if we push on the concepts a little, we see that each of these also subdivides. I must leave the subdivisions of logical consequence for another day, although I think it is a very deep and very important fact that, in the Western European tradition, causal reasoning has exactly the same structure as deductive logic. What I want to focus on here are the subdivisions of causal consequence. There appear to be at least two different ways of thinking about causality. Each of these corresponds to a distinct narrative syntax. And each syntax in turn appears to characterize a distinct species of ethical thought.

Inheritors of a seventeenth-century Western European way of thinking about causation tend to think of *things* as billiard balls and to think of *events* as billiard-ball trajectories. Causes are trajectories that result in impacts: the whack of one billiard ball against another makes the second ball move off in a predictable way. If you have lots of billiard balls and they're all in motion, things can get complex, but the idea is that, in principle, and if you have enough information, you can *calculate* what's going to happen. Causes and effects are connected by straight, or at least calculably curved, lines.

But in some other cultures (and even at some times and in some places in Western European culture), causality is seen in terms both less linear and less discrete: events are understood to cluster, to form ecologies, rather than lining themselves up like railway schedules. This is the conception of causality that underlies the *Yi Jing,* for example, as well as Carl Jung's notion of 'meaningful coincidence.' If you want to know the consequence of some action or state of affairs, you don't attempt to discern a linear order in which the action has a determinate place; rather, you ask, "What *sorts* of events or situations tend to hang together with this *sort* of event or situation?" 'The cause' is no single item, no single billiard-ball whack. A 'cause' and an 'effect' are understood as interrelated aspects of some organic state of affairs.

To illustrate the difference, consider possible responses to the question "Why is it snowing?" On the first, billiard-ball, model of causality, someone might answer by saying that, owing to the temperature of the air at a certain elevation, the molecules of water vapour began to freeze and, as they froze, they formed crystals when they became attached to submicroscopic particles suspended in the atmosphere, etc., etc. On the second, ecological, model, the question might be answered by saying, "It's January, and we're north of the 53rd parallel." That is, one appeals to meaningful co-occurrence, to the fact that things and events sometimes hang together in a net or a cloud of ontological weather.

How does the distinction play out in terms of narrative syntax? The billiard-ball conception corresponds to what, for lack of a better term, I will call *straight-line* or *lineal* narrative syntax. The second, the ecological conception, corresponds to the narrative syntax of many myths and dreams — to what I'll call *oneiric* syntax (after the Greek word *oneiros,* or *dream*). The logic governing oneiric syntax was mapped for post-Enlightenment audiences by Freud in the late nineteenth and early twentieth centuries. He called it 'primary process' and characterized its two fundamental features, *condensation* and *displacement*. In condensation, an image can be telescoped, compressed, or abbreviated. In displacement, it can be carried by, in, around, or under another image that is associated with it in some way, including being its opposite. Thus, in primary process thought, images and events are not subject to what we might call the daylight orders of Western European logical and causal consequence. Dreams and myths, as I've mentioned, are characterized by this type of thinking.

Straight-line narrative syntax, on the other hand, underlies what we generally think of as reportage. It is basic to the idea of a 'systematic' or 'informed' account. For example: "Chinese troops crossed the border today into X. Russia responded by stalking out of an emergency UN Security Council meeting, while the Chinese press hailed General Y as a defender of the spirit of cooperation. World oil prices fell by 30 cents a barrel as it became clear X would offer no resistance to the Chinese takeover. X is currently the world's third largest producer of synthetic crude." *Because* (in the Western European sense) the troops crossed the border, the Russians were upset. *Because* no resistance was offered, world oil prices fell. The cue strikes a billiard ball, and that ball in turn strikes another. The order of presentation in such a report is fundamental to articulating the particular causal connections the speaker wishes to convey. Compare: "World oil prices fell today by 30 cents a barrel. Russia responded by stalking out of an emergency UN Security Council meeting, while Chinese troops crossed the border into X, which is currently the world's third largest producer of synthetic crude." This is a different story. While prolepsis and flashback allow the presentation of events in a narration to differ from their order in experience, such devices nonetheless affirm the presence, in reportage, of a 'standard' or 'normal' order of presentation: we could not define prolepsis and flashback, nor discern their workings, if this were not so.

Accounts of achievements in engineering, indeed most descriptions of technological workings, like post-seventeenth-century romance and history, tend to be sub-species of the lineal genre. Although many of us assume the same is true of science, Arthur Koestler has argued that in offering lineal reconstructions of the development of Enlightenment science we are misrepresenting what occurred. When looked at carefully, many noteworthy discoveries appear to have an oneiric logic. (Think of the stories surrounding the discovery of Archimedes' principle, or August Kekulé's discovery of the molecular structure of benzene, or Michael Faraday's conception of electric and magnetic fields, or Albert Einstein's vision of relativity.) It is perhaps truer to say that Western European culture likes to represent science to itself as a lineal activity — the fount of technological wisdom that gives humans control over nature.

To understand a narrative whose syntax is lineal is to grasp that certain events are triggered by others. To understand a narrative with oneiric syntax is, by contrast, to grasp that certain types of events form families; they 'hang with' one another. Think about the bank advertisement that shows a smiling woman, man, girl, and boy: it doesn't matter who's in the foreground, who's been partly cropped out of the picture: we read 'family' (even when it crosses our mind that they're all models and probably not related to one another). And, in this culture, the *image* 'family' often hangs together with the *image* 'home in suburbia' — the bank is counting on this — along with various other images like 'high school graduation,' 'steady job,' and 'apple pie.' Houses in suburbia don't *cause* apple pies; steady jobs don't *cause* high school graduations — but the images cluster together in one culturally sanctioned 'account' of happiness.

Imagine a group of event-types constellated in this way: marriage, death, and rebirth, say. Marriage, in certain Greek and Irish myths, involves a kind of psychic death, especially for women; and rebirth is consequent on this death. Does marriage then cause psychic death? Does death cause marriage? Does either cause rebirth? Not in a straight-line sense. But life — or stories — can teach people that such events hang together.

Here are some examples.

Myth one: A hero must descend a well to retrieve the ring of youth; the heroine sees that he cannot do this without killing her and climbing down on her bones; so she offers herself, he follows her instructions, and then he reassembles the bones, placing the ring over her heart so she will live again. Later, when he is required to choose a bride, he recognizes her hand in the dark by its crooked little finger — a bone he did not set quite right.

Myth two: During the marriage feast for a king, a slighted goddess fills the groom's bed with snakes, demanding his death; the goddess's brother makes a deal with the Fates — if anyone will die in the groom's place, he may live; the groom's aged parents and his best friend refuse, so his bride steps forward; she dies, but is soon rescued from Hades by a hero. In Euripides' version, when she returns from Hades, she must be silent for three days.

Myth three: A queen prays for the birth of a girl; her wish is granted, but the price is the transformation of her seven sons into swans; the queen dies and the king, mad with grief over the loss of his sons, abandons the girl in a hut in the woods; the swans come and tell her that if she undertakes to weave them shirts of nettle, in complete silence, she can redeem them; she agrees; a prince rides by, sees her, falls in love; he marries her, but she never speaks or laughs or cries — she behaves as one dead — and keeps weaving. Only with the birth of her own child, stolen from her and, she believes, killed, is she herself transformed: she cries out in grief, the shirts shrivel to old leaves, the swans fly off, and she tells her husband who she is.

All three stories are saying that female death, rebirth, and marriage come with their hands linked. Standard causal orders and daylight logic — which proscribe resurrection, beds suddenly full of snakes, and talking swans — are overthrown *in order* to tell us this. But most of us don't react as though we've been told something merely fantastical, nor as though we've been handed a string of non-sequiturs. The lineal order of events is impossible, but intuitively, we sense some other, very important, form of connectedness at work. And because the lineal order is impossible, up to a point, that order doesn't matter; this is why we're able to recognize these three accounts as versions of the same oneiric narrative.

The question of how we distinguish narrative with oneiric syntax from lists of non-sequiturs is a deep one. At its root is the phenomenon of gestalt comprehension, our perception of things as wholes with interdefined parts. (That is, Gestalt theorists argue, we do not perceive independent elements or atomic 'parts' and 'sum them up' into recognizable entities. We perceive wholes first, and their parts later.) Our faculty of gestalt comprehension can indeed be exercised on strings of unconnected items, and, if directed to do so, will often produce what Sharon Mesmer has described as "a little pop in [the] mind" — the shadow of the experience of genuine understanding. This is what happens, for example, when people use a randomizing selection device of some sort on an existing text ("Select only the words that contain the letter t") and tell us the result is poetry. If we stare at it long enough, many of us will feel we get it. (Sort of.) Does it follow from this that 'genuine understanding' doesn't really exist, or that there is no 'external' world that genuinely hangs together in numerous ways? No. It follows that we must learn, and practise, epistemological discernment.

What do these observations about straight-line and oneiric narrative syntax tell us about ethics?

The word 'ethics' comes from the Greek word *ethos*, meaning a set of customs or traditional ways of living that define a cultural community. To be 'ethical' in this root sense means to be 'one of us.' And there appear to be at least two ways in which such ethical wisdom is commonly communicated. It is often communicated as a set of rules or commandments — Mosaic law is an example. Even more often, however, it is communicated through the telling of stories. Stories, of course, figure in the Judeo-Christian ethical tradition, but in many oral cultures, stories constitute the core of the ethical tradition: a certain phrase or a proverb can be used to bring a story quickly to mind, but there is no explicit table of commandments.

It is hard for some of us — at least it has been hard for me — to begin to get a feel for what it would be like to acquire an understanding of an *ethos* mostly through stories. I was brought up, as most of us were, in a local, as well as general, cultural context laden with dos and don'ts. I was exposed only haphazardly to stories in the Bible, and not at all to those in any other major religious text. I was an avid reader of Greek myths in Nathaniel Hawthorne's versions, but although I found them beautiful, they were not a part of the lives of any people I had dealings with, and so they remained unintegrated in my own. It was only in later years, as I made serious friends, that stories began to assume what I see in retrospect was an ethical dimension in my life. We might meet, two or three of us, for coffee and to talk; one of us might be in trouble; another would say, "Oh, I know about that! When I was living in ..." and *tell a story*, with elements or an ending that echoed the situation of the one in trouble. These stories — unlike the injunctions offered by my family, my community, and my school — communicated empathy, the recognition that the troubled person was seeking to regain equilibrium, that they wanted the good but couldn't see their way to it in the present situation. Although the stories were never of epic proportions, and although their syntax was often that of reportage, their insights were not presented as prescriptive maxims; no one tried to lay out a summary statement of what anyone in such a situation ought to do. The echoic elements in the accounts were attempts to sketch common features in the landscape, and thereby to offer perspective without judgement. This, I now see, communicated a respect for the autonomy of the troubled person, as well as confidence in their desire for the good. And so I am led to speculate that such respect for autonomy and confidence in human nature may be characteristic of cultures that voice their ethics primarily or exclusively through stories.

The absence of the imperative mood, the absence of a maxim that draws the moral of the story, can be a feature of any narrative, however. So the way in which it inspires autonomy and communicates confidence in human nature is not a function of either oneiric or lineal syntax. Indeed, in cultures that generally prefer to convey their ethical teaching through stories rather than prescriptive maxims, stories with both (and often mixed) narrative syntaxes are plentiful. Oral cultures often draw the distinction between the relevant narrative genres in terms of time: myth-time and a noticeably oneiric structure go together, while historical time and a predominantly lineal structure go together. What *is* a function of syntax is the *way* in which the imperative mood is, or may be, absent. In the lineal case, it is, or can be, absent as a matter of fact; in the oneiric case, it is essentially absent.

For the oneirically structured story *actively* resists translation into precepts. To the extent that such translation is possible, what one gets are not prescriptive maxims, but very general ontological claims: "The world has ears" or "Nature loves to hide"; "Birth, death, marriage: the three big events in a woman's life are one event" or "For every action, there is an equal and opposite reaction." Better, longer, translations would sound like interpretations of dreams. Such accounts, like dreams themselves, rarely involve telling anyone what to do. They say: *Here is your situation. Expect this, or perhaps this, and perhaps this, too.* If there is a recommendation, it is to be alert: to listen; to attend to the deep structures in your life, the motivic patterns of being, and to align yourself with them. *That is the most, that is all, you can do.* The ethical teaching contained in an oneiric narrative helps its auditors learn the lay of the ontological land: it is *understood* that any normal person will incline to a harmonious relationship with it. Myths are metaphysics, ontology, ethics, and aesthetics rolled into one. Because their syntax is fundamentally oneiric, the ontology they conjure is one of resonant interconnectedness; and because of this, what rests within the stories is often, or significantly, an ethics of integrity — an attempt to foster interior and environmental alignment. This is most pronounced in the case of pre-agricultural myths; in Neolithic and Bronze Age myths — those of the *Odyssey*, for example — there is an admixture of attempts to master, or at least to outwit, nature. And in significant measure, the good life in myths from societies with large-scale agriculture is still understood to involve coping, in a decorous way, with forces beyond one's control. Even in myths of the industrial age we find this view, though it is often couched negatively: in Goethe's *Faust* and Shelley's *Frankenstein*, for example, or indeed in George Lukas's *Star Wars*, the failure to curb our appetite for control precipitates disaster.

Consider, by contrast, ethical thinking that is at home in a lineal narrative. Keith Basso describes the *'ágodzaahí* ('historical tales') of the Western Apache — which are distinguished from *godiyįh-go nagoldi'é* (myths) — as "morality tales pure and simple." Their grammar is predominantly lineal, and they are told, according to

Basso, to effect moral correction. Like the ethical teachings in many Judeo-Christian stories, they contain advice on what a good person ought, or mostly ought not, to do if they wish to be welcome in human society: don't meddle, don't act like a whiteman, don't commit incest. (Do share wealth, do respect your mother-in-law, do remain loyal.) And while there are crucial differences between the ethical attitude that informs the act of telling a story and that which informs uttering a commandment, there is also a crucial similarity: lineal narratives and prescriptive moral maxims are built around the same conception of causality, a conception of causality that *enables* prescription: "Do X, and Y will happen." When it is structured in this way, the prescriptive moral maxim becomes the epitome of lineal causal thought. And the agenda with which it is allied is not the fostering of interior and environmental alignment: it is the imposition, from without, of community standards for acceptable social behaviour.

This, then, is the fundamental difference between ethics conditioned by lineal syntax and ethics conditioned by oneiric syntax: lineal narrative ethics — albeit obliquely at times, albeit in a generic way — tell you what the culture expects of you; oneiric narrative ethics don't.

But are things ever this clear-cut? Earlier, I said that in many oral cultures there were stories with differing narrative grammars. And certainly in Judeo-Christian, Islamic, and Hindu cultures, there are myths as well as lineal narratives and prescriptive maxims. And while Judeo-Christian and Islamic scriptures, by and large, do not contain the panoplies of oneirically structured narratives that populate pagan thought, they nonetheless do contain myths as well as lineal narratives and maxims. (One powerful oneiric narrative that appears in these texts, in numerous guises, is the myth of the *causelessly* rejecting or punishing father — the bad dream of just not being able to get it right.) What good, then, is a theoretical distinction that shows up, on the ground, as a mixed bag?

Its virtue lies in enabling us to discern emphases within a given culture, and so to begin to understand that culture's moral style. It's true that pure cases may not exist in any tradition. We thus should perhaps envision a spectrum of ethical insights and teachings, with prescriptive maxims, as quintessential lineal narratives, at one end, and oneiric narratives, with few or at least non-prescriptive precepts, at the other. Ethical thinking that inclines towards expression in a lineal syntax will tend to embody a notion of the good life as life in accordance with a set of social constraints. Ethical thinking that inclines towards expression in oneiric syntax, on the other hand, will embody a notion of the good life as harmonious attunement, both internal and external. Moral teaching in the lineal mode will aim at instruction and correction, while in the oneiric mode it will amount to providing individuals with maps — or, better, to humming the theme with the main chord changes underneath, so that any human who happens to be listening in can start to figure out how to sing along.

Ontological Attention and Lyric Form

There are, however, ethical gestures that seem to resist translation not only into maxims but into any sort of guiding narrative. Recall Vedran Smailović playing Giazotto's Adagio in G Minor at the Sarajevo bomb site every day at 4:00 p.m. for twenty-two days. There is a rudimentary narrative — I've just given it — but it suggests nothing about what anyone else ought to do, nor does it describe a cluster of events that others ought to expect. From what I have read, Smailović did not regard himself as an exemplar; he did not believe everyone ought to undertake to make a similar gesture; nor did he think bomb sites in general were archetypally attended by music-making. Doing that, there, then was what *he* felt compelled to do. "Exactly," someone might say, "and that's what shows the gesture was not particularly moral. It was a private act of mourning." Except it wasn't private; it was remarkably public. At the heart of its public nature was the fact that Smailović had no strong personal connection with any of the dead. This is what made the gesture so potent: it was an act of witness.

We tend to think of witness as something people do in connection with events about which they feel badly; horror, tragedy, and injustice are the sorts of things we stereotypically say we 'bear witness to.' Is witness, then, essentially an attempt to shame perpetrators, a kind of finger-pointing? While grief at some wrong often attends an act of witness, attempts to shame or blame do not seem to comprehend their full meaning. Think of Smailović's gesture: grief and outrage, certainly; but what arrests us is its integrity as a *testament*. Laying blame is overshadowed by a struggle to state the truth. Outrage, grief, the wish to blame are partly why one has to struggle, and a being that did not feel them would not be human. But the point is not *simply* to scream and weep together. The point is to scream and weep for the right reasons. Those reasons are something like: *This happened. See: a real life. See: a real death. See: reality.*

That is: witness attends to being. By which I mean that it attends not so much to a billiard-ball-like string of events and individuals, but to a resonant whole in which individual things and events are experienced as interdefined aspects of that whole. This alerts us to the possibility that the focus of witness may not always be horror and injustice. In her notebooks, Simone Weil speaks of an "immense responsibility" to "testify as an apple tree in blossom testifies, or as the stars do." To what does the apple tree testify? Weil describes it as the presence of the divine in the material world; or we might borrow from Dylan Thomas and say that it testifies to the force that through the green fuse drives the flower. We don't usually think of such witness as ethical precisely because straight-line notions of justice get no purchase in such situations: nothing that can be described as a crime has been committed. But witness, like oneiric narrative, is concerned with our attunement to the whole. Positive witness understands that we have a duty to praise, and that it is this duty that underlies the witness of mourning. Cheerfulness is a virtue not just because it makes us pleasant company for other humans — the straight-line perspective — but because it reflects a genuine grasp of the most fundamental fact of the matter: things exist. The witness of grief is the complement of our ability to stand before this fact in joyful astonishment.

But if witness is fundamentally an act of attention to the resonant ecology of the world, in what sense is it ethical? And in what sense is it 'non-narrative'? Surely some of the most compelling testaments in Western literature are novels — Coetzee's *Age of Iron*, for example, Pasternak's *Doctor Zhivago*, Anne Michaels's *The Winter Vault*. Indeed. But the extraordinary power of these novels does not lie in the structure they share with journalistic reportage. It lies in what they share with lyric poetry.

Witness is ethical because it *enacts* responsibility. It does not presume to tell anyone else what to do — from its perspective, the world is too complex, individual contexts are too multiple and multi-faceted, to support blanket prescriptions for action. Witness does not even demand discernible gestures of mourning or celebration. What it demands is the acknowledgement that would allow such gestures to be genuine. *See,* it says, *they were. See,* it says, *this is!* Witness is pre-eminently a form of insight.

As I have already suggested, it is rooted in being struck by existence — that *isness* is, that individual beings are, that they stand in tense but resonant relation, and that both suffering and delight are real. Recognitions of this sort typically do not take the form of precepts — they are neither general nor abstract. Instead, we are, as Wittgenstein says, *pierced* by some being or by its situation. The emotion attendant on being struck in this way is a kind of love; we might call it, following Don McKay, ontological applause — except that applause is sometimes too noisy a reaction for the intensely inward, intimate awe that can characterize such moments.

Sometimes it is very clear to us what we ought to do following such a recognition. A few lines after the image of the apple tree, Simone Weil remarks: "The poet produces beauty by fixing his attention on something real. The act of love is produced in the same way. To know that this man, who is cold and hungry, really exists as much as I do myself, and is really cold and hungry — that is enough, the rest follows of itself." But in other cases — the Sarajevo bombing, the death of a biome caused by global warming, the praiseworthy weed flowering in tar — there is no *remedial* action available to us as there is in the case of the person who is cold and hungry. Our duty in such cases — it is perhaps the first duty in every case — is to fix our attention on the real: to see, to become aware. And then to allow what we have become aware of to work on us, to allow it to change our lives.

The moment of awakening to such awareness could, of course, be described in a narrative. A description of the consequences, may, in some cases, also happily take narrative form. But the awareness itself, which involves perception of an integrated whole, is lyric. And the expression of witness to which it gives rise — the shining testimony — must, if it is to mean what it says, take lyric form. Which brings us to the question of *Doctor Zhivago* and its cousins, the contemporary novels of witness. They are surely, by definition, stories; they are not mythic. In what sense could they possibly be said to be non-narrative in form?

The mark of a lyric novel is that it sings what it has to say: its architecture is not journalistic, nor rhetorical, nor argumentative. Isn't this true of all good novels? It is true of many. (Many good novelists began their literary careers as poets.) There are also many novels whose architecture is essentially reportorial or argumentative which nonetheless have lyric passages, or which exhibit a lyric sensibility. That is, most actual examples incorporate mixed modes, and the expression of lyric awareness need not preclude all narrative gestures. What lyric awareness requires is that the form of the gesture — whether large or small, local or architectural — be determined by deep structural metaphor, by imagistic and conceptual rhyme, by linguistic music. It is this essentially atemporal structure that allows lyric gestures to respond truly, to be enactive embodiments of lyric insight. It is how they can say, without undoing, what they mean.

In many fundamental ways, oneiric narrative syntax echoes the structure of lyric insight. Both lyric and oneiric logics reject time's arrow. Both types of gesture say that the orders of waking thought distort the mystery of what-is; they say that the order of the world, unmediated by human language, is not *simply* rational, linearly causal, properly grammatical, calculable, or systematic. It is not fair. Or unfair. It is resonant.

The project of making lyric gestures in language is thus acutely paradoxical. It is an attempt to effect a translation into a medium that, while capable of physically sonorous resonance, is conditioned by inhospitable grammatical constraints.

Lyric and oneiric logics are not, however, identical. One difference between them is the preoccupation, in oneiric narratives, with what Jung would call archetypes — embodiments of specific kinds of energy: sky, sea, earth, rain; princess, medicine woman, wise man, misfit. Lyric thought focusses on the resonant particular. Its genius is the perception of much larger wholes in or through such particulars. I don't mean it turns individuals into symbols — that is exactly what it doesn't do; it insists on them as individuals. But it sees them as interdefined aspects of an ecology of being. And so, when we attend to them with focus and discipline, we find a much larger world opening up.

Here's an example, a famous poem by Tang Dynasty poet Lǐ Bái. The translation is based on those by Arthur Cooper and Mike O'Connor:

ON SEEKING A TAOIST MASTER IN THE MOUNTAINS
THAT HOLD THE SKY ALOFT AND NOT FINDING HIM

>*A dog barking and the sound of running water;*
>*peach blossoms heavy with rain.*
>
>*Deep in the woods, deer at times are seen.*
>*At noon, along the stream, I hear no bell.*
>
>*Wild bamboos cut across mist on green slopes;*
>*flying cascades hang from jade peaks.*
>
>*No one knows where you've gone!*
>*I lean against one pine, then another, then another!*

The poem does employ tropes; but it is also extremely vivid. You can hear the silence, except for the dog and the stream — those elusive deer. You can feel the altitude — those flying cascades. When I was trying to think of a poem that presented the natural world with great clarity, this one sprang to mind although I hadn't read it in twenty years.

The poem says: *I went to find the master and he wasn't there!* How frustrating! It says, simultaneously, in the same space, with the same words: *I went to find the master and found the natural world.* The simultaneity of these two thoughts is the meaning of the poem. The theme is a common one in Zen poetry. But if the images were all clichés or symbols, the poem wouldn't work: it is the intense *presence* of the world that gives the poem its power. Note that there is only one human being in the poem: the one that doesn't get it.

Straight-line narrative, I suggested earlier, supports the idea that ethics consists of prescriptions, a list of *dos* and *don'ts*. Ethical maxims do embrace time's arrow; they root themselves in billiard-ball-style causal linkages, and the failures and successes of individual egos. Straight-line moral narrative gives us a sense of security. We use it to reassure ourselves that things stand in orders that we can, in principle, control. Lyric, by contrast, knows that the world is not controllable, that its individuals belong to a vast, intricate, overwhelming, integrated whole. The supreme moral virtue, according to lyric thought, is attentiveness. Acts of witness change us as dreams do: we are re-oriented, we feel reality shift, or rather feel ourselves erased, opened to the unlanguageable beauty and terror of what-is.

> *Once, after the rain, I walked from town,*
> *by the seedpod fences, along the rammed earth of a road*
> *on which double tyre-marks shone*
> *far into the cellular afternoon....*
> *I came out on a hillslope above the lilac ocean.*
> *Light on the clouds opposite sunset*
> *was like that in the foyer of a seashell.*
> *White eucalyptus rose about me in front of the sea, their leaves*

like long green parakeets.
The mind easily fragments within such dimensions: I felt it poise
far above, a second, as I was leaning
there, on the moist, thin rind
which is all that is delicacy, all that's edible fruit,
of this country. Then I realized how probably the land
I had just walked over was already owned
in some boardroom of Hong Kong or Japan. And all I'd just seen
became things that lay in a fire
in the moment when they still have their form.

— ROBERT GRAY,
from "Under the Summer Leaves"

Frost and Snow

I was sitting on the floor in front of the wood stove one evening late in 2007 when I realized my vocation for teaching had disappeared. One moment it was there, the next it had vanished. At the time, I put this down to the sudden intrusion of an image: the sea of laptops my classroom had recently become. I had resolutely refused to sign on to the digital revolution (even now I do not own a cell phone or have a social media account) and the influx of laptops suggested to me that I would be unable to communicate with this new generation of students. Not because I was failing to use PowerPoint, but because the analogies on which my teaching style depends would not reflect the culture's new obsessions. Pretending that I shared those obsessions wouldn't work — you can't fake that sort of thing. I saw immediately that this loss of vocation meant that I would have to leave the university; and I felt dismay.

My dismay sprang from the sense that I would thereby be giving up on politics. For I viewed, and still view, the teaching of philosophy (and history and literature) as an intensely political activity. At the root of all serious engagement with what we now call the humanities is the question *What is the good life?* Stimulating interest in that question, stoking the courage required to sustain reflection, is, I still believe, the only way to arouse a passion for justice. And I thought that awakening that passion in individuals, grounding it there in insight, discernment, and empathy, was the only secure route — narrow, but real — to a better, less abusive, less exploitative, polity.

Do I still believe such a polity is possible? I write on the cusp of a dissolution of that faith. Why awaken the soul to justice if the only result can be to increase awareness of the futility of aspiring to justice in the world? Plato's answer is that the acquisition of justice correctly conceived — justice as a right ordering of the intellectual, combative, and appetitive elements of the soul — allows one to bear the futility of politics. But I do not believe this notion of justice adequately captures our intuitions. My own intuitions, at any rate, coincide in a general way with John Rawls's: justice is fairness. And I believe that a passion for justice involves delight in fairness for its own sake, not simply because fairness gets you more of what the fat cats presently have. It depends on an instinct for empathic consideration of situations not one's own, not merely on dispassionate assessment of ways to realize one's interests or to keep the state stable. Ordering one's own soul so that it can withstand mistreatment by one's fellow citizens is a noble aspiration, and one to which I subscribe. But it does not strike me as the acquisition of justice; it strikes me as the acquisition of means to cope with injustice.

In addition to dismay at the recognition that I was no longer capable of meaningful engagement in the classroom, I also felt relief. I did not acknowledge this at the time, but the rapidity, the seamlessness, the joy with which I made the transition to life outside the academy, pointed to it. And as I reflect, I realize that that relief meant the trouble had started before the laptops.

~

If you have spent any time in a university classroom built after the Second World War, you will recognize the one I left: a low ceiling of wood-waste panels; fluorescent lighting; cinder-block walls with a thick coat of beige, green, or yellow paint; beige linoleum on the floor; if you're lucky, a strip of windows in narrow aluminum frames; an untidy array of plastic bucket chairs, each with a little laminated pressboard panel on which it is possible to balance either a book or a notebook (or a laptop), but not both; at the front, a chalkboard (usually green) and often, though not always, chalk; and between the chalkboard and the plastic bucket chairs, an ever-expanding array of apparatus for 'digitizing' the classroom.

I believe Plato's Sokrates was right about philosophic method: the first step is learning to think critically about one's inherited opinions — learning to discern that they *are* opinions rather than unquestionable truths; and the second step is learning how to search for solid epistemological ground — how to distinguish good questions from silly ones, how to weigh conflicting intuitions and to understand their roots. I believe Plato's Sokrates was also right about the engine driving the second step: it's *eros,* the ungainsayable pull of beauty. It's because we can tell the good life is beautiful that we're able to sustain the hard work of achieving it: if we cannot see its beauty, we descend into skepticism, an eviscerating cynicism about the possibility of meaningful experience. I'm not suggesting that the classroom itself constitutes the good life, though that is an old ideal; I'm suggesting that if the place where we try to conduct philosophical conversation is a routine and unrelenting assault on the senses, this, in and of itself, demands extra energy of the participants. They must cut through the overburden of cultural acquiescence in bad design, must reach through it to a sensitivity that, in order to cope with the phenomenological assault, has been buried.

~

Pierre Hadot, in "Philosophy as a Way of Life," asks: "Does the philosophical life, then, consist only in the application, at every moment, of well-studied theorems, in order to resolve life's problems?" As the rhetorical structure of the question indicates, his answer is no. He offers an analogy between adopting philosophy as a way of life and artistic creation: "It may seem as though artists, in their creative activity, do nothing but apply rules, yet there is an immeasurable distance between artistic creation and the abstract theory of art. In philosophy, however, we are not dealing with the mere creation of a work of art: the goal is rather to transform *ourselves*." In other words, we are attempting to induce a conversion experience. I disagree with the suggestion that art aims at the "mere" transformation of materials. Artists, in my experience, are often attempting to respond to the arrival of insight: a sudden, sharp awareness of meaning. Although the scale of such experiences varies greatly, and many are more limited in scope than full-scale religious conversions, that is essentially what the arrival of insight is: a conversion experience. A gestalt of some part of the world shifts. One perceives anew. Art itself can precipitate such a shift in a viewer, and it can be as profound as Saul's experience on the road to Damascus. Rilke, standing in front of an Archaic torso of Apollo, knew he had to change his life. But I agree with Hadot that in attempting to stimulate genuine and sustained interest in the question *What is the good life?*, a teacher of philosophy is attempting to facilitate just such a conversion experience. Plato was clear about this: standing up and stepping away from unthinking acquiescence in the received views of one's culture means that the soul must be *turned*. This is frequently a painful business.

Why should anyone agree to undergo this transformation? Here is the mystery: no one does agree. The decision is never rational. It is forced on one. Alkibiades, in *Symposium,* voices his astonishment: "A kind of *madness* comes over me when I listen to Sokrates. He makes me feel that my life — *my* life! a life of fame, glory, power, luxury, and the instant gratification of every appetite — is shameful." That is, inexplicably, Alkibiades' gestalt of the world undergoes a profound shift in Sokrates' presence. How are such shifts induced? There are many ways: physical abuse, emotional abuse, sustained lying, creating an addiction. None of these, however, is involved in the shift Alkibiades experiences. What happens to Alkibiades is like the shift Rilke experiences: he *sees* Sokrates' moral integrity and in the same instant, knows it for the most beautiful thing he has ever seen. He falls in love.

Love, they say, is blind. What is usually meant by this is that erotic desire, rooted solely in another's physical appearance, can lead us to overlook or deny characterological faults — cruelty, greed, a manipulative style, a tendency to lie. That's why both Plato and Xenophon stress Sokrates' physical ugliness and his lack of social grace: physical beauty and winning ways are not the source of his charisma. Nor is it swagger. Cameron Anderson and his colleagues have shown that human beings repeatedly fall for overconfident males, even when those males demonstrably lack the competence they claim; but Sokrates is more like a dishevelled gumshoe than he is like Donald Trump. All he knows is that he doesn't know much, except about *eros*. What attracts people, against their habitual preferences, is Sokrates' integrity. Our love for this kind of beauty, Plato claims, is the opposite of blind. It leads us to see things, including ourselves, as they really are. Love of integrity produces a shift in our vision of what matters; it shows us what we really want — a kind of security that wealth and fame cannot begin to match. This shift — an awakening to our situation — makes us begin to pay attention to the world.

Are there any guarantees that insight will arrive? That the conversions we undergo will be true? There are none.

This does not mean that all conversions are to false understandings of reality, nor that we cannot, over time, evaluate them accurately.

~

My own office was not bad: bare brown brick walls instead of painted cinder block; tough brown wall-to-wall instead of linoleum; and a window, at desk height, that ran the entire width of the west wall and looked out into a large greenspace in the centre of campus. But the demands of the bureaucracy were exploding, both as a result of, and enabled by, the shift to 'information technology.' Every month or so there was a new (cumbersome, unintuitive) electronic form or survey designed to increase my accountability. Class sizes were exploding, too. When I first taught an upper-level course in Plato in the mid-'90s, it enrolled 22 students — too many, given that Plato's conception of philosophy involves one-on-one psychogogic conversation rather than lecture-style instruction, but we managed. By the mid-'00s, I was being asked to teach two sections of 60 students each. I had argued the proposed cap on my environmental philosophy course from 120 down to 90. And then there was the status of environmental philosophy itself: it was, and still is, regarded by the philosophical industry as an 'applied' rather than a 'pure' sub-discipline, the sort of course you might offer to the university student body at large, but with which majors are not expected to concern themselves. The idea of such 'service' courses is that they provide clarifications of real-life ethical dilemmas by taking a 'philosophical approach' to them. But a serious attempt to come to grips with an honest syllabus for such a course will reveal that the challenge flows in the reverse direction, from the nature of environmental problems to our conception of philosophy. For the arid hegemony of analysis in the English-speaking tradition and the anthropocentric preoccupations of the post-Kantian poststructuralist tradition are epistemological *symptoms* of the environmental crisis; neither embodies a method for solving it. It's an irony that would not have been lost on the author of *Euthyphro,* but one with which I was making little headway in the profession. The pay was great; the pay was staggering. But it wasn't the job I'd signed on for. I now see that my sense that I wouldn't be able to communicate with the laptop-obsessed was simply the most recent addition to a gravitationally challenged pile. It was the whole thing that had collapsed, quite suddenly, that night by the fire. The relief I felt was the relief that comes from ceasing to hold an increasingly distorted posture.

But what was I going to do to make ends meet? I'd grown up on a farm. My plan was to leave the city and hire out as a gardener while reserving part of my time to write. Where to go was solved, as my spouse already lived in a rural community; it was in front of his wood stove that I'd realized my days in the academy were done. As it turned out, I didn't have to hire out as a gardener. I got enough work as a freelance writer, editor, and lecturer to supplement a bit of royalty income. But I did get serious about growing food.

≈

Hadot writes that for the ancients philosophy "was a method of spiritual progress ... a way of life which brought peace of mind (*ataraxia*), inner freedom (*autarkeia*), and a cosmic consciousness." By "cosmic consciousness" he means "consciousness that we are a part of the cosmos, and the consequent dilation of our self throughout the infinity of universal nature." I'd prefer "the consequent dissolution of the self in the intense interconnectedness of nature," but the basic goal — harmonious coexistence with other-than-human beings — is one that I salute. Living closer to the land has deepened my sense of the fragility and resilience of all beings. One is made daily, effortlessly grateful to be alive.

What, though, of politics?

With constant awareness of death and birth, of flourishing and disease, with physical work, outside, in all weathers, comes not only "cosmic consciousness" but also a certain peace of mind. (At least, in the absence of crises. There are usually several in any given season, but realizing one has survived many and knowing one won't survive them all, helps one to maintain perspective.) Inner freedom, though — freedom from concern about what others may think or do, freedom from concern about what may befall beings that I love — continues to elude me. I have not been able to let go of my desire to see justice in the world. In particular, I have not been able to muster indifference to the fact that members of my species — not just a handful of overconfident males, but the billions glad to see them in power, the billions spoiling for a fight, the millions among the rich and educated who regard overconsumption as a right and will not contemplate restraining their desire to reproduce — are destroying the beauty, the harmony, on which all life depends. I am filled with disbelief, with outrage and despair.

How dare they.

~

In 2018 Karen Stenner and Jonathan Haidt published research indicating that "about a third of white respondents across ... twenty-nine liberal democracies proved to be authoritarian to some degree." In a subsequent interview, Stenner provided the following gloss on 'authoritarian': "a deep-seated, relatively enduring psychological predisposition to prefer — indeed, to demand — obedience and conformity." She continued: "So the classic conditions that typically activate and aggravate authoritarians — rendering them more racially, morally, and politically intolerant — tend to be perceived loss of respect for / confidence in / obedience to leaders, authorities and institutions, or perceived value conflict and loss of societal consensus / shared beliefs, and/or erosion of racial/cultural/group identity. This is sometimes expressed as a loss of 'who we are' / 'our way of life.'" This, of course, was meant to help explain Trump's continuing popularity despite his lying, his cheating, his impeachments, his farcical behaviour on the world stage, and his wholesale disregard for the day-to-day well-being of his supporters (to say nothing of his sexism, his willingness to court racists, and his aspirations to permanent office). But it explains with equal lucidity Sokrates' state execution on fake charges in 399 BCE — and dovetails very precisely with Eric Havelock's diagnosis in his 1952 essay "Why Was Socrates Tried?" We do not know the size of the jury, but it was likely 501. If Plato's statement in *Apology* is correct — that "a switch in only thirty votes" would have acquitted Sokrates — then 55 per cent voted for condemnation. Considerably more than a third, but not much more than supported Trump in 2016 and 2020. James Pogue's "The Art of Losing," published in the August 2020 issue of *Harper's,* makes no reference to Stenner and Haidt's research, but it presents compelling anecdotal evidence that loss of a sense of 'who we are' drove (and, we might surmise, continues to drive) support for Trump.

Reflecting on these observations, I have begun to wonder if Richard Rorty is not right. Perhaps the teaching of philosophy cannot hope to ameliorate injustice, and should not be regarded as anything more than a project of edification. I note that Stenner and Haidt used data only from persons whom their survey technique identified as "white." But what if their conclusion pertains to us all? If somewhere between a third and half of us are characterologically attracted to authoritarian social structures, then there's no point trying to awaken in everyone a passion for equal opportunity, due process, or the integrity whose achievement is the goal of a philosophic way of life. And for the remaining half or two-thirds? They may appreciate, as I have appreciated, contact with the scintillating, generous, challenging minds whose traces are available in the library; but exposing them to these sources of inspiration will make little difference to the present polity and certainly will not affect the course of history. In some periods, things will change for what some of us feel is the better; but the numbers on the other side mean that it won't take much to tip the scale in the other direction. Enjoy what you can while the wheel of Fortune turns. And follow Epikouros in his principled shunning of politics.

Dù Fǔ, in the eighth century CE, wrote a poem which in Kenneth Rexroth's translation reads:

> It is late in the year;
> Yin and Yang struggle
> In the brief sunlight.
> On the desert mountains
> Frost and snow
> Gleam in the freezing night.
> Past midnight,
> Drums and bugles ring out,
> Violent, cutting the heart.
> Over the Triple Gorge the Milky Way
> Pulsates between the stars.
> The bitter cries of thousands of households
> Can be heard above the noise of battle.
> Everywhere the workers sing wild songs.
> The great heroes and generals of old time
> Are yellow dust forever now.
> Such are the affairs of men.
> Poetry and letters
> Persist in silence and solitude.

This is a brilliant indictment of attempts to effect political reform. The evidence that there's no point trying is the poem itself: that it speaks to us across twelve centuries and from a wholly different culture. It is also evidence that poetry and letters do persist alongside human injustice and violence. If you're male. If you're female, you likely weren't taught to read and write. If you were, your work was likely disparaged or lost or misattributed or you were beaten and locked in your room when you tried or you quit making it when you got married. I can abjure politics and read Plato, but not Aspasia. I can locate many scores by recherché male composers, but not important ones by Lili Boulanger, or Elizabeth Maconchy, or Rebecca Clarke, despite the prizes they won when they were alive a few decades ago. John Glubb, in *The Fate of Empires,* noted that the rise of women in the professions immediately preceded the collapse of the Roman Empire, the collapse of the Abbasid Caliphate, and the collapse of the British Empire. Empires may not be political structures in which we should acquiesce, but they remain dominant features of the global political landscape. Such are the affairs of sexually dimorphic anthropoid primates.

≈

Two years before I left the university, I lost the land on which I grew up. My mother needed to move to the city for health reasons and my spouse would not contemplate joining me on the farm. It's one of the hardest decisions I've made. The land was my true parent; it had not only provided the food, air, and water that made the cells of my body, it had also been my refuge and my comfort, gentle, strong, and steadfast, when the humans around me were unable to be those things.

I was therefore utterly astounded by my experience the last time I walked the west field. It was summer, late evening; I was preoccupied with sorrow, choked by the sense I had betrayed my truest friend. And up from the ground, up through the soles of my boots, came the awareness — clearer than speech, like a hand on my shoulder — that the land felt no betrayal, that it loved me and was glad for me to go, that its energy was wild and boundless, unconstrained by human decisions or desire. It is the fact that I couldn't comprehend what I was sensing — or rather that I comprehended it, but couldn't *imagine* it — that convinced me what I was picking up was genuine. In that moment, I touched the most potent, the most enduring form of inner freedom. It was not mine. But I was still able to recognize it: a love so enormous, so exuberant that it was unaffected by my failures, or by any of its own possible fates. And I realized I'd been afforded a glimpse into what it is, really, to *be*.

≈

Those of us alive now, those of us in whose lifetimes the earth's human population has exploded from a sustainable 2.5 billion to 8 billion-and-counting, those of us in whose lifetimes something could have been done to halt the exploitative juggernaut that is driving the climate cataclysm and a sixth mass extinction, we will not live to know whether we merely signed the death warrants of many human cultures, or the death warrant of our species along with those of countless others, or if we managed to allow the destruction of complex life on the planet. Regardless, it's a lot of blood on a lot of hands. And those of us who saw the threat before it was too late, who tried, who tried for decades, either through mass politics or through attempts to turn one soul at a time, are we not entitled to a little despair? Plato, we note, did despair. His last dialogue, *Laws,* is the gesture of a thinker who has given up trying to persuade humans to be good. If he couldn't bear it, how shall we? Moreover, laying down rules, as Plato does in *Laws,* never works in the long run. It merely produces one more turn of Fortune's wheel, different faces on top, different heads rolling below.

Despair, it is said, presumes too much. It is ungrateful for the fact that we still draw breath. It takes the self too seriously. It pretends to know that beauty and being both can, and will, die. It is graceless.

I should like not to be graceless or ungrateful. Still: what good did it do to teach? What good has it done since to write? Or to try to live a sustainable life?

Today I received a package in the mail. I didn't recognize the name on the return address label. In the package was a number of poems, records of sudden shifts of insight about oak trees, about the author's father, about a stranger's gesture, about deer. A letter accompanying the poems told me that their author had attended a workshop I'd given several years ago and that at the time I'd encouraged her to take poetry seriously. She was writing to let me know she'd heard me, that she'd hit a bad patch for a while, but that she'd remembered, had started working on the poems again, had written some new ones. She said she wanted me to know she hadn't given up.

I'm remembering that exuberant, unfettered love that surged through the soles of my boots: the land, being. Not sensing ignorance of what might happen, nor that what might happen was irrelevant, but that everything was relevant — the pearl grey of the deer mouse's ear, the thunderhead to the northwest, the shadow of the Swainson's hawk that had earlier grazed the fence line, the new harrow parked outside the machine shed, my grief, the gold glint in the ripple on the beaver pond, the rattle in the balsam poplar's leaves. All of it, all of it, the guillotine, the drop from the helicopter, the slow live dismemberment, the scent of the wild roses on the railway bed, the coda of the second movement of Fauré's piano trio, every bit of it shot through with meaning. Even planetary ecocide, absorbed in the immensity that is being. Human moral beauty is simply one species, one version, of that ontological integrity. Species go extinct all the time. Being doesn't. Human evil is nothing more than the transient coalescence of an opposable thumb with characteristics we share with many other species: aggressiveness, territoriality, mammalian compulsion to comply, social organization in dominance hierarchies, anthropoid primate sexual dimorphism. Loss, yes, every second, irretrievable, this beauty gone for good, and gone for good someday my struggle with my desire for justice, and erased, my despair at the erasure of women's work; and newness, every second too, and new beauty, even if it's the frozen dust of Mars or the brilliance of thermophilic archaea once again spreading across the planet.

Plato's ghost, are you there? Sokrates? Do you hear? I come close some days, but I haven't given up.

Haydn's F-Flat

The structure of the coda of the Adagio of Haydn's String Quartet Op. 64 No. 3 is simple. It opens with a lilting melodic phrase in the second violin, immediately echoed by the first violin. When the second seems about to repeat the phrase for a third time, it hands the downbeat to the viola and begins a haunting triplet accompanying figure. The first violin then enters on an F, lifting to A-flat with a graceful embellishment, before falling to D and embarking on a chromatic scale that descends in measured quarter notes from D-flat to A. It lifts briefly to a B-flat again and resolves, through A-flat, to G. The same sequence, minus the first few bars of traded melody, is then repeated an octave lower. In the second statement, the cello, rather than the second violin, introduces the accompaniment, but every other note in the following six bars is identical. With one exception. This time, the first violin enters on an F-flat, which it sustains, unembellished, for a full three eighths.

F-flats are rare in the Western European canon, and are especially rare before the nineteenth century. You need them only when you are moving in remote areas of diatonic tonality or, as here, when you want to construct a highly unusual chord. (This one appears to be a Neapolitan sixth, with striking extensions.) It's not so much Haydn's chromatic daring that arrests my attention, though. It's the emotional geometry that his daring reflects.

The coda's fundamental key is E-flat major. It's a warm key, rich: late summer, honeyed light, the harvest coming in. Although the first statement of the descending scale is coloured by shifts suggesting E-flat minor, the effect of these shifts is poignant rather than disorienting. The dark falls earlier, there's frost in the air — we know this. The relation between the two keys is the relation between praise song and elegy: nothing lasts forever, winter follows autumn before turning back to spring. Sorrow is inextricably bound up with our capacity for love.

The F-flat in the restatement says *no, you didn't quite understand*: there will be no warm fireside. Spring won't come — at least, not in a form you recognize. Your grief will be beyond tears. Loss at the limits of the imagination.

And love? The first violin figure rises to A-flat again, as it did the first time, then drops to D. The scale steps down in the shifting light. In the final three measures, the cello holds unwaveringly to the tonic, the other three voices rising and falling gently within the key, fading, fading. At the limits of vision, winking out.

* * *

Acknowledgements

My sincere thanks to the individuals, audiences, and editors who read or listened to initial versions of many of these essays, and who offered discerning commentary. I am especially grateful to Roo Borson for her generous attention to the manuscript as a whole, and to Robert Bringhurst, Laurie Graham, Warren Heiti, and Colin Macleod for their comments on early drafts of individual essays. The late Daniel Bryant's assistance with the translation of the poem by Xiè Língyùn, which appears in "Lyric Realism," was essential to the project. And I'm very grateful to Phil Carlsen, Harald Krebs, Allie Picketts, Jeffrey Ryan, and Bruce Vogt for musicological discussion of Haydn's F-flat. Many thanks to Khadija Coxon and Kathleen Fraser at the Press, and to two anonymous referees, whose generous and encouraging commentary facilitated the book's development. Jane McWhinney's superb eye and her comprehensive insight into what I was trying to achieve were invaluable in preparing the final manuscript.

~

The publisher and author acknowledge, with thanks, permission to reprint the following copyrighted material:

⁋ Excerpts from *Poetry and the Sacred* by Don Domanski (Nanaimo: Institute for Coastal Research, 2006), quoted by kind permission of the Literary Estate of Don Domanski. (The text is reprinted in *Selected Poems 1975–2021*, Scottish Borders: Corbel Stone, 2021.) ⁋ An excerpt from "Under the Summer Leaves" in *Selected Poems* by kind permission of the author, Robert Gray. ⁋ Excerpts from "New World Northern: Of Poetry and Identity" in *Plummets and Other Partialities* by Ralph Gustafson, reprinted by permission of Sono Nis Press. ⁋ Two excerpts from "I'm Explaining a Few Things" in *Selected Poems* by Pablo Neruda, translated by Nathaniel Tarn, reprinted by generous permission of the Random House Group. ⁋ Excerpts from "Traveller, Conjuror, Journeyman" in *The Filled Pen: Selected Non-Fiction* by P.K. Page, reprinted by permission of University of Toronto Press. ⁋ Excerpts from "The Integrated Life" by kind permission of the author, Sue Sinclair.

ACKNOWLEDGEMENTS

Diligent efforts have been made to discover the copyright-holder for *Evening Land / Aftonland* by Pär Lagerkvist, translated by W.H. Auden and Leif Sjöberg, published in 1975 by Wayne State University Press. The author and publisher would be grateful to be contacted by anyone with relevant information.

~

Versions of a number of essays in this book first saw print elsewhere. My thanks to the editors of the publications concerned:

⁋ "Auden as Philosopher": A version was first given as a Gustafson Lecture at Vancouver Island University in 2011. That version was subsequently published in 2012 as part of a book by the same name, by the Institute for Coastal Research, Nanaimo, British Columbia. ⁋ "Wilderness and Agriculture": *The Eye in the Thicket*, ed. Sean Virgo (Saskatoon: Thistledown Press, 2002), 187–97. ⁋ "Once upon a Time in the West": *Thinking and Singing: Poetry and the Practice of Philosophy*, ed. Tim Lilburn (Toronto: Cormorant Books, 2002), 187–99. ⁋ "Lyric Realism": *The Malahat Review* 165 (Winter 2008): 85–91. ⁋ "The Ethics of the Negative Review": *The Malahat Review* 144 (Fall 2003): 54–63. ⁋ "Integrity and Ornament": *Crime and Ornament*, ed. Bernie Miller and Melony Ward (Toronto: YYZ Books, 2002), 205–16. ⁋ "The Novels of Pascal": *Brick* 32 (Winter 1988): 25–31. ⁋ "'Being Will Be Here'": Sections of this essay originally appeared in the introduction to *Hard Choices: Climate Change in Canada*, ed. Harold Coward & Andrew J. Weaver (Waterloo: Wilfrid Laurier University Press, 2004), 1–10. ⁋ "A Note on Jane Jacobs's *Systems of Survival*": *Brick* 105 (Summer 2020): 48–53. ⁋ "On Rules and Moral Beauty": *50 Years of Freedom: A Festschrift Celebration for the Golden Anniversary of the BC Civil Liberties Association*, ed. Kate Milberry (Vancouver: BC Civil Liberties Association, 2013), 114–17. ⁋ "Lyric, Narrative, Memory": *A Ragged Pen: Essays on Poetry & Memory* (Kentville, Nova Scotia: Gaspereau Press, 2006), 85–105. ⁋ "Frost and Snow": *Brick* 107 (Summer 2021): 45–53.

Notes

◀ AUDEN AS PHILOSOPHER: HOW POETS THINK

page 3 — *what Ludwig Wittgenstein called 'seeing as'*: Wittgenstein [1958] 1972: Part II, §xi, esp. pages 193–208.

page 4 — *Duck-rabbit*: The figure is a version of Joseph Jastrow's duck-rabbit (familiar to those who know the work of Ludwig Wittgenstein): Jastrow 1900, 295. Jastrow reports that the drawing in his own text is "[f]rom *Harper's Weekly*, originally in *Fliegende Blätter*."

— *Necker cube*: See Necker 1832.

— *Pythagorean theorem*: The proof shown here is only one of many. It requires seeing that the two large squares are identical in area (both have sides of length $a + b$), and the four triangles in each are also, cumulatively, identical in area. Thus the remaining areas — the square with sides of length c in the first diagram and the two smaller squares in the second diagram, with sides of lengths a and b respectively — must also be identical.

page 5 — *as Max Wertheimer pointed out*: Wertheimer 1959, Ch. 1. See also Wertheimer 1925 and his essay "The Syllogism and Productive Thinking" in Ellis 1938, 274–82.

— *Wertheimer also stressed the importance of 'hearing-as'*: Wertheimer 1959, Conclusion and Appendix 1. The recognition that melodies are gestalts predates Wertheimer and may be found in von Ehrenfels 1890.

— "*The kingfisher chortles ...*": Bringhurst [2001] 2009.

— *The objects of the imagination, [Auden] tells us, are "encountered,"* etc.: Auden [1956] 1989, 54–5.

page 6 — *The terms ... are borrowed from Coleridge*: Coleridge [1817] 1965. See Ch. XIII, concluding paragraphs.

— *The Primary Imagination, according to Auden...* : Auden [1956] 1989, 54.

page 6   "a passion of awe": Auden [1956] 1989, 55.
—   "from joyous wonder to panic dread": Auden [1956] 1989, 55.
—   *Sacred beings are themselves various*: Auden [1956] 1989, 55.
—   *Primary Imaginations differ*: Auden [1956] 1989, 56.
—   "every imagination responds to those it recognizes in the same way": Auden [1956] 1989, 55.
—   "sacred to all imaginations": Auden [1956] 1989, 55.
—   "[t]he realm of the Primary Imagination is without freedom, sense of time or humour": Auden [1956] 1989, 55.
—   *other key claims in the section as a whole*: Auden [1956] 1989, 51, 60, 56.
—   "self-forgetful": Auden [1956] 1989, 56.
—   *what Freud calls ... "primary process"*: Freud elaborates the notion of primary process in numerous places throughout his work. See, for example, Freud [1900] 1958, Freud [1915] 1957, and Freud [1911] 1958. Freud [1895] 1966 is particularly interesting, as it constitutes the first and fundamental formulation of the idea, though the manuscript remained unpublished in Freud's lifetime.

page 7   *Charles Rycroft ... has linked it*: Rycroft 1975.
—   *Auden, as a number of his reviews and his famous elegy attest*: "Sigmund Freud," "The Greatness of Freud," "The Freud-Fliess Letters" and "The History of an Historian" in Auden 2008, 340–4, 385–8, 472–7, 596–601 respectively; and Auden [1939] 2007.
—   *As Graham Greene remarked*: Greene 1971, 185.
—   *It attends ... "not [to] the sacred and the profane ..."*: Auden [1956] 1989, 56.
—   *what Freud termed "secondary process"*: Freud [1900] 1958, Freud [1911] 1958. See also Freud [1895] 1966, §[15] The Primary and Secondary Processes in Ψ.
—   "we cannot both help agreeing ...": Auden [1956] 1989, 57.

page 8   "craves agreement with other minds": Auden [1956] 1989, 57.

NOTES TO PAGES 9–16

—	"a bourgeois nature …": Auden [1956] 1989, 57.
page 9	"the inspiration of sacred awe": Auden [1956] 1989, 57.
—	"deliberately and ostentatiously different": Auden [1956] 1989, 58.
—	"Even when it employs the diction and rhythms of conversation …": Auden [1956] 1989, 58.
page 10	*poetry is* "intimate": Auden [1956] 1989, 54.
page 11	ROBERT BRINGHURST: Bringhurst 2007, 15–16.
pages 11–12	DON DOMANSKI: Domanski 2006, 7–8 & 14–15. Also in Domanski 2021, 295–6 & 302–3.
page 12	RALPH GUSTAFSON: Gustafson 1987, 87, 88, 94.
—	DENNIS LEE: Lee 1998, 180.
—	TIM LILBURN: Lilburn 1999, 6. Lilburn is, in a way, responsible for a number of the remarks collected here. In the early 1990s, he wrote to several poets, asking them "What does poetry know and how does it know it?" The book that resulted, *Poetry and Knowing* (Lilburn 1995), saw the first publication of the essays by Bringhurst, Lee, McKay, and Michaels.
pages 12–13	DON MCKAY: McKay 2001, 26.
page 13	ANNE MICHAELS: Michaels 1995 in Lilburn 1995, 180.
—	P.K. PAGE: Page [1970] 2007, 44 & 47.
—	SUE SINCLAIR: Sinclair 2009, 43 & 44.
page 15	*Wallace Stevens and P.K. Page have drawn a similar distinction*: See Stevens 1997, esp. 846. Page made remarks to this effect at a reading at The Black Stilt, Victoria, BC, some time between 2006 and 2009.
—	"das Schöne ist nichts …": Rilke [1923], lines 4–5. The debate about the nature of beauty has a long history in the Western philosophical canon; there are some, for example, who would argue that Rilke's view echoes aspects of Kant's notion of the sublime, a notion that Kant himself distinguished from beauty. I propose not to explore such distinctions here.
page 16	*Baconian science*: See, for example, Bacon [1605] 1975 or Bacon [1620] 1962, Book IV, *Novum Organum*.

page 16   *Descartes*: See Descartes [c. 1625–28 etc.] 1966 and [1637] 1965.
page 17   *There has been considerable debate about these issues*: For the view that many features of technocratic excess can be traced to Bacon himself, see Horkheimer and Adorno [1944/1947] 2002, Merchant 2003, and Merchant 1980. For the view that Bacon intended only a healthy interaction between humans and their environment, see, for example, Pérez-Ramos 1988 or Martin 2005. An excellent contextualization of Bacon's thought, which outlines the scholastic dogma and narrow religious piety he was attempting to remedy, may be found in William A. Armstrong's introduction to Bacon [1605] 1975.
page 19   *Novum Organum*: There are a number of editions and abridged versions. See, for example, Bacon [1620] 1962, Book IV.

◀ WILDERNESS AND AGRICULTURE

page 23   "the end of nature": McKibben 1989.
page 25   "Most of our problems began…": Herriot 2000, 142.
page 28   *Anaximander*: See Kahn [1960] 1994, 166; or Diels-Kranz [1951] 1996.

◀ ONCE UPON A TIME IN THE WEST

page 29   *Heidegger and Primal Speech therapy*: For the theses concerning being and language discussed in this essay, see Heidegger [1935–36 etc.] 1972 and Heidegger [1947] 1976. A summary of these ideas is provided in Inwood 1999 in the entries "being: an introduction" (26–8), "*Being and Time*" (28–31), and esp. "poetry and Dichtung" (168–70). See also Arendt 1978, 179–84.
page 33   *what [Being] wants to do is go'n hide*: See Heidegger [1954] 1990.

page 36   "dampness and richness of the soil," "the loneliness of the field-path as the evening falls," "the silent call of the earth, its quiet gift of the ripening grain," "uncomplaining anxiety as to the certainty of bread," "the wordless joy of having once more withstood want": Heidegger [1935–36 etc.] 1972, 23 & Heidegger 1993, 159.

page 37   *Shelley and poets having had it with unacknowledgement*: Shelley [1821, 1840], last sentence.

—   *Plato denying poets legitimacy as thinkers*: Plato 1961 & 1997. Republic X, 595a–608b.

◀ LYRIC REALISM: NATURE POETRY, SILENCE, AND ONTOLOGY

page 40   *Konrad Lorenz ... remarks*: Lorenz 1977, trans. Ronald Taylor, 14–15.

—   *David Abram ... writes*: Abram 1997, 63–5.

pages 41–2   "Climbing Green-cliff Mountain in Yǒngjiā" by Xiè Língyùn: My sincere thanks to the late Daniel Bryant for assistance with the translation. See also Frodsham 1967 and Hinton 2001.

page 43   *With Freud...*: See, for example, Freud [1911] 1958.

—   *There is considerable evidence...*: See, for example, the testimonies on pp. 11–13.

—   *Herakleitos*: Diels-Kranz [1951] 1996: Fr. 51.

page 44   *etymology of kin*: Klein 1971.

◀ THE ETHICS OF THE NEGATIVE REVIEW

page 56   "Works of art are of an infinite loneliness ...": Rilke 1932 (third letter, 23 April 1903), 18–19. In English translation, Rilke 1962, 29.

◀ INTEGRITY AND ORNAMENT

page 59   *Epigraph*: Adolf Loos [1910] 1962, 315.

—   "Ornament and Crime." Loos [1908] 1962.

—   "our cultural level": Loos [1908] 1962, 286; "the Papuan," 276; "the negro," 277; "laggards" ... *such as Tyrolean peasants*, 280; "aristocrats," 286. In English translation, Loos [1929] 1998, 167, 170, 173.

—   ADOLF LOOS: "We do not sit ...": Quoted in Paul Engelmann's unpublished collection *Bei der Lampe*, in Janik and Toulmin 1973, trans. Janik and Toulmin, 99.

page 60   EGON FRIEDELL: "These rooms ...": Friedell 1932, trans. C.F. Atkinson, 299–300.

page 61   *Image*: 'Grecian Vase' Toilet, J.L. Mott Iron Works, New York, in Gerhard 1897, Fig. 394, 179.

page 62   *Allan Janik and Stephen Toulmin argue persuasively...*: Janik and Toulmin 1973.

—   KARL KRAUS: "Adolf Loos and I ...": Kraus [1918] 1955, 341. Trans. Janik and Toulmin in Janik and Toulmin 1973, 89.

—   EGON FRIEDELL: "This brings us ...": Friedell 1932, trans. C.F. Atkinson, 300–1.

page 63   "organically bound up with": Loos [1908] 1962, 283. See Loos [1929] 1998, 171.

page 64   *gestalt intelligence*: For a more detailed characterization, see Zwicky 2019a.

—   *as a gestalt stands to the sub-gestalts that it embraces*: For elaboration, see Zwicky 2019b, 68–9.

—   *lyric*: See Zwicky 2015.

—   *we learn that 'sense organs' do not passively register 'sense data'...*: The seamless interdependence of 'perception' and 'cognition' is amply demonstrated by lesion studies: profound distortions in our registration of reality result from insult to parts of the brain not directly involved in the 'transmission' of 'stimuli.' See McGilchrist 2009, Ch. 2; Luria 1973 & 1980. Max Wertheimer's so-called 'factors' of *Gestalt* perception — which affect perception of arrays, collectivities, partial figures, and the like — are further evidence of the interdetermination of perception and thinking. See Wertheimer 1923; Metzger 1936; Wagemans *et al* 2012. The epistemological interdetermination is so profound that it has led some to propose ontological interdetermination. See McGilchrist 2009, Ch. 4; Merleau-Ponty 1945; Abram [1996] 1997.

page 65   CALL FOR SUBMISSIONS, *Crime and Ornament*: For Miller and Ward 2002.

page 66   "Beauty is boring": personal communication from a postmodern artist.

page 68   ADOLF LOOS: Loos [1910] 1962, 314–15.

page 70   HERAKLEITOS: Diels–Kranz [1951] 1996: Fr. 49a.

◀ THE NOVELS OF PASCAL

Those unfamiliar with the work and reputation of Thomas Bernhard will find an overview in Cousineau 2001. Both the *Encyclopedia Britannica* (1949) and *The Encyclopedia of Philosophy* provide overviews of Pascal's life and works.

◀ BEING WILL BE HERE, BEAUTY WILL BE HERE, BUT THIS BEAUTY THAT VISITS US NOW WILL BE GONE

page 85   *Title*: Bringhurst [2005] 2009, staves 88–9.
page 86   *As for Me and My House*: Ross 1941.
page 87   *The archaeological record suggests...*: Walker 1988.
—   *current interglacial... coming to an end*: Pielou 1991, esp. 12–15.
—   *suggested to John Macoun in 1879 that European-style agricultural settlement could be sustained there*: Herriot 2000, 154–5. Herriot compares reports of three early European visitors to the region, noting differences in rhetorical style that may also have influenced the Canadian government's decisions to promote European colonization

of the region. The three accounts in question are to be found in Palliser 1859, Hind 1971, and Macoun 1882.

page 88   "one-in-a-thousand-years event": For example: Jeff Berardelli, "Pacific Northwest Bakes under Once-in-a-Millennium Heat Dome," CBS News, 29 June 2021, or Jade Prévost-Manuel, "Heat Wave Would Have Been 'Virtually Impossible' without Climate Change, Report Suggests," CBC News, 7 July 2021. Reports in the media referred to research reported by World Weather Attribution in "Western North American Extreme Heat Virtually Impossible without Human-Caused Climate Change," 7 July 2021. The conclusion of the World Weather Attribution initiative was disputed by Cliff Mass, a professor of atmospheric science at the University of Washington, in "Was Global Warming the Cause of the Great Northwest Heatwave? Science Says No," *Cliff Mass Weather Blog,* 5 July 2021. The WWA analysis was defended by Mark Buchanan in Buchanan 2021. See also Jonathan Watts, "World 'Must Step Up Preparations for Extreme Heat,'" *The Guardian,* 7 July 2021, for an overview that situates the 2021 Pacific northwest heat dome in the context of other extreme weather events.

page 90   *We were told in the '60s*: In 1965, US president Lyndon Johnson's Science Advisory Committee issued a report, *Restoring the Quality of Our Environment,* that warned about the warming effects of rising carbon dioxide levels. See "Section I. Carbon Dioxide from Fossil Fuels — The Invisible Pollutant," 112–33, esp. 121–4 & 126–7.

—   *A number of recent articles*: See, for example, Banerjee 2015, Hall 2015, Schlanger 2015, Carrington and Mommers 2017, Franta 2018, Freedman 2018, Milman 2023.

—   *there's a time lag between emissions and effects*: See, for example, Rood 2017.

—   *The Precautionary Principle ... surfaced in discussions of environmental degradation as early as the '70s*: Boehmer-Christiansen 1994, see esp. 35–8. Although the phrase 'precautionary

> principle' does not appear in Arrow and Fisher 1974, a version of the concept is discussed there with reference to environmental harms.

page 91 *David Suzuki was saying we had until the early '90s to turn things around*: personal memory.

— *emissions are on the rise again*: International Energy Agency 2021.

page 92 "Being will be here …": Bringhurst [2005] 2009, staves 88–9.

— "The things of which there is seeing, hearing, and perception, these do I prefer": Herakleitos: Diels–Kranz [1951] 1996: Fr. 55.

— "Nameless: the origin …": *Tao Te Ching*, Ch. 1.

page 93 *As Warren Heiti has written*: Heiti 2021, 312.

¶ A NOTE ON JANE JACOBS'S SYSTEMS OF SURVIVAL, OR WHY WE WILL NOT BE ABLE TO PREVENT GLOBAL ECOLOGICAL COLLAPSE

page 96 *The core set is the same as Plato's*: Courage is a fundamental virtue in stories from surviving pre-colonial cultures, as are self-knowledge, self-restraint, alertness, quickness of comprehension, and fair dealing. The three theological virtues of Christianity — faith, hope, and charity — are not directly echoed in pre-colonial or pre-Christian European cultures. (Charity, for example, figures strongly in Native American oral literature, but usually as something extended *to* humans by nonhumans, and less frequently as something humans bestow on others.) But Christianity's cardinal virtues — justice, fortitude, temperance, and prudence (a form of sagacity) — are an exact match for Plato's. Islam emphasizes faith and charity; but it also enjoins justice, as well as a combination of self-restraint and wisdom in a number of specific forms including humility, honesty, and trustworthiness. The rabbinical tradition in Judaism emphasizes justice and, like Islam, enjoins self-restraint in numerous specific forms. Courage is not mentioned as frequently as justice and compassion, but it is exemplified in the Tanakh. It is not mentioned in the Qur'an.

page 97   *lists of the characteristics*: Jacobs 1992, 23–4. Guardian syndrome characteristics have been re-ordered to highlight contrasts with trader syndrome characteristics.

page 98   "practical working life": Jacobs 1992, 20.

◀ ON RULES AND MORAL BEAUTY

page 103   *Kafka*: Kafka [1914–15, 1925] 1951 and 2000.
—   *Dickens*: Dickens [1852–3] 1996.
—   *As the* BC *Civil Liberties Association has said …*: Advertisement for "The Law Protecting Liberty: What You Need to Know," a course offered by BCCLA Continuing Professional Development on 2 June 2012.

◀ LYRIC, NARRATIVE, MEMORY

pages 109–10   "… Everything / loud with big voices": excerpts from Neruda [1947] 1975, trans. Tarn, 103–105 and 105–107.
page 110   *every lyric gesture is … a song of longing*: Friesen 2006, 33.
page 112   "But how describe the world seen without a self?…": Woolf [1931] 1968, 247.
page 113   Western Apache godiyịhgo nagoldi'é: Basso 1996, 49.
page 116   "A stranger am I, was a stranger born …": Lagerkvist 1975, trans. W.H. Auden and Lief Sjöberg, 113–115. Ellipses in original.

◀ THE SYNTAX OF ETHICAL STYLE

page 120   *Carl Jung's notion of 'meaningful coincidence'*: See Jung [1951] 1969 and Jung [1952] 1969, esp. par. 982 in the former.
—   *the logic governing oneiric syntax was mapped … by Freud*: Freud [1915] 1957 and Freud [1911] 1958. Oneiric syntax has

been mapped at other times and in other cultures — by Herakleitos, for example, and in the text known as the *Dào Dé Jīng*. But the cartographic styles are difficult for many twenty-first-century post-colonial readers to follow.

page 121   *Arthur Koestler has argued*: Koestler [1959] 1989.

pages 123–4   *Gestalt theorists argue...*: See, for example, Wertheimer 1925: 43, or Wertheimer, Michael 1980: 213.

page 124   "a little pop in [the] mind": Sharon Mesmer, quoted in Fischer 2009.

page 126   *Keith Basso describes...*: See Basso 1996, 49ff.

—   "morality tales pure and simple": Basso 1996, 51.

page 129   "immense responsibility" *to* "testify...": Weil 2004, 448–9.

—   *we might borrow from Dylan Thomas*: Thomas 1952.

page 130   *as Wittgenstein says,* pierced: Wittgenstein 1967, §155.

—   *we might call it, following Don McKay, ontological applause*: McKay 2001, 26.

—   "The poet produces beauty by fixing his attention...": Weil 2004, 449.

—   *praiseworthy weed*: Rich [1971] 1975, 188.

pages 133–4   "Once, after the rain,...": Gray 1990, 225–6.

◀ FROST AND SNOW

page 136   *justice is fairness*: Rawls 1971. See in particular Ch. 1 §3.

—   *Plato's Sokrates was right about philosophic method*: See, for example, Plato, *Meno* 70b–86d.

page 137   *Plato's Sokrates was also right about the engine driving the second step*: See, for example, Plato, *Symposium* 206b–212b or *Phaidros* 249b–251b.

—   "Does the philosophical life, then, consist...": Hadot 1995, 268.

—   "It may seem as though artists...": Hadot 1995, 268.

page 138   *Saul's experience on the road to Damascus*: The Bible, Acts 9: 1–18.

page 138	*Rilke ... knew he had to change his life*: Rilke [1908] 1987.
—	*Plato was clear ... the soul must be* turned: Plato, *Republic* 514a–517a.
—	*Alkibiades, in* Symposium, *voices his astonishment*: Plato, *Symposium* 215d–216c.
—	*Plato and Xenophon stress Sokrates' physical ugliness and his lack of social grace*: Plato, *Symposium* 215b, 216c–d; *Theaitetos* 143e. Xenophon, *Symposium* 4.19, 5.5–6.8.
—	*All [Sokrates] knows is that he doesn't know much...*: Plato, *Apology* 21d; *Lysis* 204c; *Symposium* 177e, 201d.
—	*What attracts people ... is Sokrates' integrity*: *Symposium* 216b–219d, 221d–222a.
page 140	*for the ancients philosophy "was a method of spiritual progress ..."*: Hadot 1995, 265.
—	*By "cosmic consciousness" he means...*: Hadot 1995, 266.
page 141	*"about a third of white respondents..."*: Stenner and Haidt 2018, 192.
—	*"a deep-seated, relatively enduring psychological predisposition..."*: Stenner 2018.
page 142	*"a switch in only thirty votes" would have acquitted him*: Plato, *Apology* 36a.
—	*Perhaps the teaching of philosophy ... should not be regarded as anything more than a project of edification*: Rorty 1980. Ch. VIII.

References

Abram, David. [1996] 1997. *The Spell of the Sensuous: Perception and Language in a More-Than-Human World.* New York: Vintage.

Anderson, Cameron. 2009. "Why Do Dominant Personalities Attain Influence in Face-to-Face Groups? The Competence-Signalling Effects of Trait Dominance." *Journal of Personality and Social Psychology* 96.2: 491–503.

Arendt, Hannah. 1978. *The Life of the Mind.* Vol. 2, *Willing.* New York: Harcourt Brace Jovanovich.

Arrow, Kenneth J. and Fisher, Anthony C. 1974. "Environmental Preservation, Uncertainty, and Irreversibility." *Quarterly Journal of Economics* 88.2 (May 1974): 312–19.

Auden, W.H. [1939] 2007. "In Memory of Sigmund Freud." In *Collected Poems.* Ed. Edward Mendelson. New York: Modern Library, 271–4.

— [1956] 1989. "Making, Knowing and Judging." In *The Dyer's Hand.* New York: Vintage, 31–60.

— 2008. *The Complete Works of W.H. Auden: Prose, Volume III, 1949–1955.* Ed. Edward Mendelson. Princeton: Princeton University Press.

Bacon, Francis. [1605] 1975. *The Advancement of Learning.* London: Athlone Press.

— [1620] [1860] 1962. *The Works of Francis Bacon.* Ed. and trans. James Spedding, Robert Leslie Ellis, and Douglas Denon Heath. Stuttgart: Friedrich Frommann.

Banerjee, Neela. 2015. "Exxon's Own Research Confirmed Fossil Fuels' Role in Global Warming Decades Ago: Top Executives Were Warned of Possible Catastrophe from Greenhouse Effect, Then Led Efforts to Block Solutions." *Inside Climate News,* 16 September 2015. https://insideclimatenews.org/news/16092015/exxons-own-research-confirmed-fossil-fuels-role-in-global-warming/, accessed 9 September 2021.

Basso, Keith. 1996. *Wisdom Sits in Places: Landscape and Language among the Western Apache.* Albuquerque: University of New Mexico Press.

Bernhard, Thomas. 1979. *Correction.* Trans. Sophie Wilkins. New York: Alfred A. Knopf.

Boehmer-Christiansen, S. 1994. "The Precautionary Principle in Germany – Enabling Government." In T. O'Riordan and J. Cameron, eds. *Interpreting the Precautionary Principle.* London: Cameron May, 31–60.

Bringhurst, Robert. [2001] 2009. "Xuedou Zhongxian." In *Selected Poems.* Kentville, Nova Scotia: Gaspereau Press, 131–2.

— [2005] 2009. "New World Suite N° 3." In *Selected Poems.* Kentville, Nova Scotia: Gaspereau Press, 201–31.

— 2007. "Everywhere Being Is Dancing, Knowing Is Known." In *Everywhere Being Is Dancing: Twenty Pieces of Thinking.* Kentville, Nova Scotia: Gaspereau Press, 15–32.

Buchanan, Mark. 2021. "The Problem of Attribution." *Nature Physics* 17, 978 (September 2021). https://doi.org/10.1038/s41567-021-01346-5.

Carrington, Damian and Jelmer Mommers. 2017. "'Shell Knew': Oil Giant's 1991 Film Warned of Climate Change Danger: Public Information Film Unseen for Years Shows Shell Had Clear Grasp of Global Warming 26 Years Ago but Has Not Acted Accordingly Since, Say Critics." *The Guardian,* 28 February 2017. https://www.theguardian.com/environment/2017/feb/28/shell-knew-oil-giants-1991-film-warned-climate-change-danger, accessed 9 September 2021.

Celan, Paul. [1959] 2002. "Tenebrae." In *Poems of Paul Celan.* Ed. and trans. Michael Hamburger. New York: Persea, 88–9.

Coetzee, J.M. 1990. *Age of Iron.* New York: Random House.

Coleridge, Samuel Taylor. [1817] 1965. *Biographia Literaria.* Ed. George Watson. London: J.M. Dent.

Cousineau, Thomas J. 2001. "Thomas Bernhard." *Review of Contemporary Fiction* 21.2: 41–70.

Dào Dé Jīng. See *Tao Te Ching.*

Descartes, René. [written c. 1625–28; circulated 1664, 1684; published 1701] 1966. *Regulæ ad directionem ingenii.* In *Œuvres de Descartes.* Vol. X. Ed. Charles Adam and Paul Tannery. Paris: Librairie philosophique

J. Vrin: Centre national de la recherche scientifique. English translation, see [1701] 1961.
— [1637] 1965. *Discours de la méthode pour bien conduire sa raison, et chercher la vérité dans les sciences.* In *Œuvres de Descartes.* Vol. VI. Ed. Charles Adam and Paul Tannery. Paris: Librairie philosophique J. Vrin: Centre national de la recherche scientifique. English translation, see [1637] 1960.
— [1637] 1960. *Discourse on Method.* Trans. Laurence J. Lafleur. Indianapolis: Bobbs-Merrill.
— [1701] 1961. *Rules for the Direction of the Mind.* Trans. Laurence J. Lafleur. Indianapolis: Bobbs-Merrill.
Dickens, Charles. [1852–53] 1996. *Bleak House.* Ed. Nicola Bradbury. Harmondsworth: Penguin.
Diderot, Denis. 1751–65. *Encyclopédie, ou, Dictionnaire raisonné des sciences, des arts et des métiers, par une société de gens de lettres.* Paris: Briasson.
— 1959. *A Diderot Pictorial Encyclopedia of Trades and Industry: Manufacturing and the Technical Arts in Plates Selected from "L'Encyclopédie, ou Dictionnaire Raisonné des Sciences, des Arts et des Métiers" of Denis Diderot.* Ed. and trans. Charles Coulston Gillispie. New York: Dover.
Diels, Hermann, rev. Walther Kranz. [1951] 1996. *Die Fragmente des Vorsokratiker.* 6th ed. Zürich: Weidmann.
Domanski, Don. 2006. *Poetry and the Sacred.* Nanaimo, British Columbia: Institute for Coastal Research. Reprinted in *Selected Poems 1975–2021.* Ed. Autumn Richardson and Richard Skelton. Scottish Borders: Corbel Stone, 2021, 295–303.
Dù Fǔ. [8th century CE]. "Night in the House by the River." Translated by Kenneth Rexroth. In Rexroth 1971, 29.
von Ehrenfels, Christian. 1890. "Über 'Gestaltqualitäten.'" *Vierteljahrsschrift für wissenschaftliche Philosophie* 14: 249–92. Available in English translation in Smith 1988.
Ellis, Willis D. 1938. *A Source Book of Gestalt Psychology.* London: Routledge & Kegan Paul.
Fischer, Shell. 2009. "Can Flarf Ever Be Taken Seriously?" https://www.pw.org/content/can_flarf_ever_be_taken_seriously, accessed 15 August 2022.

Franta, Benjamin. 2018. "Shell and Exxon's Secret 1980s Climate Change Warnings: Newly Found Documents from the 1980s Show That Fossil Fuel Companies Privately Predicted the Global Damage That Would Be Caused by Their Products." *The Guardian*, 19 September 2018. https://www.theguardian.com/environment/climate-consensus-97-per-cent/2018/sep/19/shell-and-exxons-secret-1980s-climate-change-warnings, accessed 9 September 2021.

Freedman, Andrew. 2018. "Shell Knew Truth of Global Warming in 1980s; Foresaw a Hurricane Sandy Scenario: It Wasn't Just Exxon That Knew the Truth about Global Warming Way Before Many Members of the Public Did." *Mashable*, 5 April 2018. https://mashable.com/article/shell-knew-truth-on-global-warming-1980s, accessed 9 September 2021.

Freud, Sigmund. [1895] 1966. "Project for a Scientific Psychology." In *The Standard Edition of the Complete Psychological Works of Sigmund Freud*. Edited and translated by James Strachey. Vol. 1, 281–387. London: Hogarth.

— [1900] 1958. *The Interpretation of Dreams*, §VII E. In *The Standard Edition of the Complete Psychological Works of Sigmund Freud*. Edited and translated by James Strachey. Vol. 5. London: Hogarth.

— [1911] 1958. "Formulations on the Two Principles of Mental Functioning." In *The Standard Edition of the Complete Psychological Works of Sigmund Freud*. Edited and translated by James Strachey. Vol. 12, 213–26. London: Hogarth.

— [1915] 1957. *The Unconscious*. In *The Standard Edition of the Complete Psychological Works of Sigmund Freud*. Edited and translated by James Strachey. Vol. 14, 159–215. London: Hogarth.

Friedell, Egon. 1931. *Kulturgeschichte der Neuzeit: Die Krisis der europäischen Seele von der Schwarzen Pest bis zum Ersten Weltkrieg*. Band 3. München: C.H. Beck.

— 1932. *A Cultural History of the Modern Age*. Vol. III. Trans. Charles Francis Atkinson. New York: Alfred A. Knopf.

Friesen, Patrick. 2006. "Memory River." In *A Ragged Pen: Essays on Poetry*. Kentville, Nova Scotia: Gaspereau Press, 2006, 33.

Frodsham, J.D. 1967. *The Murmuring Stream*. Kuala Lumpur: University of Malaysia Press.

Gerhard, William Paul. 1897. *Entwässerungs-Anlagen Amerikanischer Gebäude. Fortschritte auf dem Gebiete der Architektur: Ergänzungshefte zum Handbuch der Architektur,* No. 10. Stuttgart: A. Bergsträsser.

Ginzburg, Carlo. 1980. "Morelli, Freud, and Sherlock Holmes: Clues and Scientific Method." Trans. Anna Davin. *History Workshop Journal* 9: 5–36.

Glubb, John. 1978. *The Fate of Empires and Search for Survival.* Edinburgh: Blackwood & Sons.

Gray, Robert. 1990. "Under the Summer Leaves." In *Selected Poems.* London: Angus & Robertson, 214–26.

Greene, Graham. 1971. *A Sort of Life.* London: The Bodley Head.

Gustafson, Ralph. 1987. "New World Northern: Of Poetry and Identity." In *Plummets and Other Partialities.* Victoria, British Columbia: Sono Nis, 87–99.

Hadot, Pierre. 1995. "Philosophy as a Way of Life." In *Philosophy as a Way of Life.* Ed. Arnold I. Davidson. Trans. Michael Chase. Oxford: Blackwell, 264–76.

Hall, Shannon. 2015. "Exxon Knew about Climate Change Almost 40 Years Ago: A New Investigation Shows the Oil Company Understood the Science Before It Became a Public Issue and Spent Millions to Promote Misinformation." *Scientific American,* 26 October 2015. https://www.scientificamerican.com/article/exxon-knew-about-climate-change-almost-40-years-ago/, accessed 9 September 2021.

Havelock, Eric. 1952. "Why Was Socrates Tried?" In *Studies in Honour of Gilbert Norwood* (*The Phoenix* Supplementary Volume No. 1), ed. M.E. White. Toronto: University of Toronto Press: 95–109.

Hegel, G.W.F. [1807] 1952. *Phänomenologie des Geistes.* Ed. Johannes Hoffmeister. Philosophische Bibliothek Bd. 114. Hamburg: Felix Meiner.

— [1807] [1952] 1977. *Hegel's Phenomenology of Spirit.* Trans. A.V. Miller. Oxford: Oxford University Press.

Heidegger, Martin. [written 1935–36] [1950] 1972. "Der Ursprung des Kunstwerkes." In *Holzwege.* 5th ed. Franfurt am Main: Klostermann, 7–68. English translation by Alfred Hofstadter under the title "The Origin of the Work of Art" in Heidegger 1993, 139–212.

— [1947] 1976. "Brief über den Humanismus." In *Wegmarken*. 2nd ed. Frankfurt am Main: Klostermann, 311–60. English translation by Frank A. Capuzzi under the title "Letter on Humanism" in Heidegger 1993, 212–65.

— [1954] 1990. "Die Frage nach der Technik." In *Vorträge und Aufsätze*. 6th ed. Pfullinger: Neske, 9–40. English translation by William Lovitt under the title "The Question Concerning Technology" in Heidegger 1993, 307–63.

— 1993. *Basic Writings*. Rev. ed. Ed. David Farrell Krell. Various translators. New York: HarperCollins.

Heiti, Warren. 2021. *Attending: An Ethical Art*. Montreal: McGill-Queen's University Press.

Herakleitos. Fragments in Diels, Hermann, rev. Walther Kranz [1951] 1996.

Herriot, Trevor. 2000. *River in a Dry Land: A Prairie Passage*. Toronto: Stoddart.

Hind, Henry Youle. 1971. *Narrative of the Canadian Red River Exploring Expedition of 1857 and of the Assiniboine and Saskatchewan Exploring Expedition of 1858*. Vol. 1. Edmonton: Hurtig.

Hinton, David. 2001. *The Mountain Poems of Hsieh Ling-yün*. New York: New Directions.

Horkheimer, Max and Theodor Adorno. [1944/1947] 2002. *Dialectic of Enlightenment: Philosophical Fragments*. Ed. Gunzelin Schmid Noerr. Trans. Edmund Jephcott. Stanford: Stanford University Press.

Hume, David. [1748] 1955. *An Inquiry Concerning Human Understanding*. Indianapolis: Bobbs-Merrill. §VII.

The I Ching or Book of Changes. [10th–2nd centuries BCE] 1950. Trans. Cary F. Baynes from the Richard Wilhelm German translation. Bollingen Series XIX. Princeton: Princeton University Press.

International Energy Agency. 2021. "CO_2 Emissions — Global Energy Review 2021 — Analysis." https://www.iea.org/reports/global-energy-review-2021/co2-emissions, accessed 9 September 2021.

Inwood, Michael. 1999. *A Heidegger Dictionary*. Oxford: Blackwell.

Jacobs, Jane. 1992. *Systems of Survival: A Dialogue on the Moral Foundations of Commerce and Politics*. New York: Random House.

Janik, Allan and Stephen Toulmin. 1973. *Wittgenstein's Vienna*. New York: Simon & Schuster.

Jastrow, Joseph. 1900. *Fact and Fable in Psychology*. Boston: Houghton, Mifflin.

Jung, Carl. [1951] 1969. "Appendix: On Synchronicity." In *The Structure and Dynamics of the Psyche*. In *Collected Works*, Vol. 8. 2nd ed. Trans. R.F.C. Hull. Bollingen Series XX. Princeton: Princeton University Press, pars. 969–97.

— [1952] 1969. "Synchronicity: An Acausal Connecting Principle." In *The Structure and Dynamics of the Psyche*. In *Collected Works*, Vol. 8. 2nd ed. Trans. R.F.C. Hull. Bollingen Series XX. Princeton: Princeton University Press, pars. 816–968.

Kafka, Franz. [1914–15, 1925] 1951. *Der Prozess*. New York: Von Schocken.

— [1914–15, 1925] 2000. *The Trial*. Trans. Idris Parry. Penguin Modern Classics.

Kahn, Charles H. [1960] 1994. *Anaximander and the Origins of Greek Cosmology*. Indianapolis: Hackett.

Kant, Immanuel. [1781] [1787] 1968. *Kritik der reinen Vernunft*. In *Werke*, Bde. 3 & 4. Berlin: de Gruyter.

— [1781] [1787] 1933. *Immanuel Kant's Critique of Pure Reason*. Trans. Norman Kemp Smith. London: Macmillan.

Klein, Ernest. 1971. *A Comprehensive Etymological Dictionary of the English Language*. Amsterdam: Elsevier.

Koestler, Arthur. [1959] 1989. *The Sleepwalkers*. London: Arkana.

Kraus, Karl. [1918] 1955. "Zeit." In *Nachts*. In *Beim Wort genommen*. In *Werke*, Vol. III. Munich: Kösel-Verlag, 339–63.

Lǎo Zi. [6th century BCE? 4th century BCE?]. See *Tao Te Ching*.

Lagerkvist, Pär. 1975. "With old eyes I look back." Trans. W.H. Auden and Leif Sjöberg. In *Evening Land / Aftonland*. Detroit: Wayne State University Press.

Lee, Dennis. 1998. "Poetry and Unknowing." In *Body Music*. Toronto: Anansi, 179–96.

Lǐ Bái. [8th century CE] 1973. "On Visiting a Taoist Master in the Tai-T'ien Mountains and Not Finding Him." In *Li Po and Tu Fu*. Trans. Arthur Cooper. Harmondsworth: Penguin.

— 1987. "On going to see a Taoist master in the Tai-T'ien Mountains but not finding him." Trans. Mike O'Connor. In Mike O'Connor, *The Basin: Life in a Chinese Province: Poems & Translations*. Port Townsend, Washington: Empty Bowl, 27.

Lilburn, Tim, ed. 1995. *Poetry and Knowing*. Kingston, Ontario: Quarry.

— 1999. "How To Be Here?" In *Living in the World As If It Were Home*. Dunvegan, Ontario: Cormorant Books, 1–23.

Loos, Adolf. [1908] 1962. "Ornament und Verbrechen." In *Sämtliche Schriften*, Vol. 1, *Trotzdem 1900–1930*. Ed. Franz Glück. Vienna: Verlag Herold, 276–88. Loos [1929] 1998 is an English translation of a later, abridged version of this essay. Note: No second volume of *Sämtliche Schriften* was issued.

— [1910] 1962. "Architektur." In *Sämtliche Schriften*, Vol. 1, *Trotzdem 1900–1930*. Vienna: Verlag Herold, 302–18. Note: No second volume of *Sämtliche Schriften* was issued.

— [1929] 1998. "Ornament and Crime." In *Ornament and Crime: Selected Essays*. Ed. Adolf Opel. Trans. Michael Mitchell. Riverside, California: Ariadne Press, 167–76. The German original of 1929 is an abridged version of Loos [1908] 1962.

Lorenz, Konrad. 1977. *Behind the Mirror: A Search for a Natural History of Human Knowledge*. Trans. Ronald Taylor. London: Methuen.

Luria, A.R. 1966. *Higher Cortical Functions in Man*. 2nd ed. Trans. Basil Haigh. New York: Basic Books.

— 1973. *The Working Brain: An Introduction to Neuropsychology*. Trans. Basil Haigh. New York: Basic Books.

Macoun, John. 1882. *Manitoba and the Great North-West*. Guelph: World Publishing Company.

Martin, Catherine Gimelli. 2005. "The Feminine Birth of the Mind: Regendering the Empirical Subject in Bacon and His Followers." In *Francis Bacon and the Refiguring of Early Modern Thought: Essays to Commemorate The Advancement of Learning (1605–2005)*. Ed. Julie Robin Solomon and Catherine Gimelli Martin. Aldershot, UK: Ashgate.

McGilchrist, Iain. 2009. *The Master and his Emissary: The Divided Brain and the Making of the Western World*. New Haven: Yale University Press.

McKay, Don. 2001. "Baler Twine." In *Vis à Vis: Fieldnotes on Poetry and Wilderness*. Kentville, Nova Scotia: Gaspereau Press, 11–33.

McKibben, Bill. 1989. *The End of Nature*. New York: Random House.

Merchant, Carolyn. 1980. *The Death of Nature*. San Francisco: Harper & Row.

— 2003. *Reinventing Eden*. New York: Routledge.

Merleau-Ponty, Maurice. 1945. *Phénoménologie de la perception*. Paris: Gallimard.

— 2012. *Phenomenology of Perception*. Trans. Donald A. Landes. Abingdon: Routledge.

Metzger, Wolfgang. 1936. *Gesetze des Sehens*. Frankfurt am Main: W. Kramer. Translated as *Laws of Seeing* by Lothar Spillman et al. Cambridge, Massachusetts: MIT Press, 2006.

Michaels, Anne. 1995. "Cleopatra's Love." In Lilburn 1995, 177–83.

— 2009. *The Winter Vault*. Toronto: McClelland & Stewart.

Miller, Bernie and Melony Ward, eds. 2002. *Crime and Ornament: The Arts and Popular Culture in the Shadow of Adolf Loos*. Toronto: YYZ Books.

Milman, Oliver. 2023. "Revealed: Exxon Made 'Breathtakingly' Accurate Climate Predictions in 1970s and 1980s." *The Guardian*, 12 January 2023. https://www.theguardian.com/business/2023/jan/12/exxon-climate-change-global-warming-research, accessed 14 January 2023.

Necker, L.A. 1832. "Observations on Some Remarkable Optical Phenomena Seen in Switzerland; and on an Optical Phenomenon Which Occurs on Viewing a Figure of a Crystal or a Geometrical Solid." *London and Edinburgh Philosophical Magazine and Journal of Science* 1.5 (November): 329–37.

Neruda, Pablo. [1947] 1975. "Explico algunas cosas" ("I'm Explaining a Few Things"). In *Selected Poems*. Ed. Nathaniel Tarn. Trans. Nathaniel Tarn. Harmondsworth: Penguin, 102–7.

Page, P.K. [1970] 2007. "Traveller, Conjuror, Journeyman." In *The Filled Pen: Selected Non-fiction*. Toronto: University of Toronto Press, 43–7.

Palliser, John. 1859. "Papers relative to the expedition by Captain Palliser of that portion of British North America which lies between the Northern Branch of the River Saskatchewan and the frontier of the United States; and between the Red River and Rocky Mountains." Paper presented to both Houses of Parliament by Command of Her Majesty: June 1859.

Pascal, Blaise. [written c. 1656–62] 1962. *Pensées*. Ed. Jacques Chevalier. Preface by Jean Guitton. Librairie générale française.

— [written c. 1656–62] 1960. *Pensées: Notes on Religion and Other Subjects*. Ed. Louis Lafuma. Trans. John Warrington. London: J.M. Dent.

Pasternak, Boris [1957] 2010. *Doctor Zhivago*. Trans. Richard Pevear and Larissa Volokhonsky. New York: Pantheon.

Pérez-Ramos, Antonio. 1988. *Francis Bacon's Idea of Science and the Maker's Knowledge Tradition*. Oxford: Clarendon.

Pielou, E.C. 1991. *After the Ice Age: The Return of Life to Glaciated North America*. Chicago: University of Chicago Press.

Plath, Sylvia. 1965. "Lady Lazarus." In *Ariel*. London: Faber & Faber, 16–19.

Plato. [fl. 4th century BCE]. 1961. *Platonis opera*. Ed. John Burnet. Oxford. Clarendon.

— *Complete Works*. 1997. Ed. John M. Cooper. Indianapolis: Hackett.

Pogue, James. 2020. "The Art of Losing." *Harper's*, Vol. 341, Iss. 2043 (August 2020): 25–34. Available online at: https://harpers.org/archive/2020/08/the-art-of-losing-kenosha-wisconsin-2020/.

Rawls, John. 1971. *A Theory of Justice*. Cambridge, Massachusetts: Harvard University Press.

Restoring the Quality of Our Environment. See United States 1965.

Rexroth, Kenneth. 1971. *One Hundred Poems from the Chinese*. New York: New Directions.

Rich, Adrienne. [1971] 1975. "When We Dead Awaken." In *Poems Selected and New, 1950–1974*. New York: W.W. Norton, 186–8.

Rilke, Rainer Maria. [1908] 1987. "Archaïscher Torso Apollos." In *New Poems* [1908]: *The Other Part*. San Francisco: North Point, 2–3.

— [1923] 1955. "Die Erste Elegie." In *Duineser Elegien*. In *Sämtlische Werke*, Vol. 1. Frankfurt am Main: Insel Verlag.

— 1932. *Briefe an einen jungen Dichter*. Leipzig: Insel-Verlag.

— [1934] 1962. *Letters to a Young Poet*. Trans. M.D. Herter Norton. New York: W.W. Norton.

Rood, Richard B. 2017. "If We Stopped Emitting Greenhouse Gases Right Now, Would We Stop Climate Change?" *The Conversation*, 4 July 2017. https://theconversation.com/if-we-stopped-emitting-greenhouse-gases-right-now-would-we-stop-climate-change-78882, accessed 9 September 2021.

Rorty, Richard. 1980. *Philosophy and the Mirror of Nature*. Princeton: Princeton University Press.

Ross, Sinclair. 1941. *As for Me and My House*. Toronto: McClelland & Stewart.

Rycroft, Charles. 1975. "Freud and the Imagination." *New York Review of Books*, 3 April 1975: 26–30. Reprinted as "Psychoanalysis and the Literary Imagination." In *Psychoanalysis and Beyond*. London: Hogarth, 1985, 261–77.

Schlanger, Zoë. 2015. "Exxon Knew about Climate Change in the 1970s, but Still Helped Block Kyoto Protocol in the '90s." *Newsweek*, 16 September 2015. https://www.newsweek.com/exxon-knew-about-climate-change-1970s-blocked-kyoto-protocol-373102, accessed 9 September 2021.

Shelley, Percy Bysshe. [written 1821, published 1840]. 1965. *A Defence of Poetry*. Indianapolis: Bobbs-Merrill. There are other editions; the essay also appears in numerous collections of and selections from Shelley's work.

Sinclair, Sue. 2009. "The Integrated Life." *Contemporary Verse 2*, Summer 2009: 43–6.

Smith, Barry, ed. 1988. *Foundations of Gestalt Theory*. Munich and Vienna: Philosophia Verlag.

Stenner, Karen. 2018. "Authoritarianism: The Terrifying Trait That Trump Triggers." Interview conducted by Tom Jacobs. *Pacific Standard*, 26 March 2018. https://psmag.com/news/authoritarianism-the-terrifying-trait-that-trump-triggers, accessed 11 November 2020.

Stenner, Karen and Jonathan Haidt. 2018. "Authoritarianism Is Not a Momentary Madness, but an Eternal Dynamic within Liberal Democracies." In *Can It Happen Here? Authoritarianism in America*. Ed. Cass Sunstein. HarperCollins, 175–219.

Stevens, Wallace. 1997. "Two or Three Ideas." In *Collected Poetry and Prose*. Ed. Frank Kermode and Joan Richardson. New York: Library of America, 839–50.

Tao Te Ching. 1993. Trans. Stephen Addiss and Stanley Lombardo. Indianapolis: Hackett.

Thomas, Dylan. 1952. "The Force that Through the Green Fuse Drives the Flower." In *Collected Poems 1934–1952*. London: J.M. Dent & Sons, 8.

United States. 1965. Restoring the Quality of Our Environment: Report of the Environmental Pollution Panel, President's Science Advisory Committee. Washington, DC: The White House.

Wagemans, J., J.H. Elder, M. Kubovy, S.E. Palmer, M.A. Peterson, M. Singh, R. von der Heydt. 2012. "A Century of Gestalt Psychology in Visual Perception: I. Perceptual Grouping and Figure-Ground Organization." *Psychological Bulletin* 138.6: 1172–1217.

Walker, Ernest G. 1988. "The Gowen Site: A Mummy Cave Occupation within the City Limits of Saskatoon." *Out of the Past: Sites, Digs and Artifacts in the Saskatoon Area*. Saskatoon: Saskatoon Archaeological Society, 65–74.

Weil, Simone. 2004. *The Notebooks of Simone Weil*. Trans. Arthur Wills. London and New York: Routledge.

Wertheimer, Max. 1923. "Untersuchungen zur Lehre von der Gestalt. II." *Psychologische Forschung* 4: 301–50. Full English translation by Michael Wertheimer and K.W. Watkins, under the title "Investigations on Gestalt Principles," in Wertheimer, Max 2012, 127–82. Abridged English translation, under the title "Laws of Organization in Perceptual Forms," in Ellis 1938, 71–88.

— 1925. "Über Gestalttheorie." Lecture for the Kant Society, Berlin, 17 December 1924. *Philosophische Zeitschrift für Forschung und Aussprache* 1: 39–60. Also published separately, Erlangen: Philosophische Akademie, 1925: 1–24. Full English translation by Kurt Riezler in *Social Research* 11.1 (1944): 78–99. Abridged translation, under the title "Gestalt Theory," in Ellis 1938, 1–11.

— 1959. *Productive Thinking*. 2nd Edition. Ed. Michael Wertheimer. New York: Harper & Row.

— 2012. *On Perceived Motion and Figural Organization*. Ed. Lothar Spillmann. Cambridge, Massachusetts: MIT Press.

Wertheimer, Michael. 1980. "Gestalt Theory of Learning." In *Theories of Learning: A Comparative Approach,* ed. G.M. Gazda and R.J. Corsini. Itasca, Illinois: F.E. Peacock, 208–53.

Wittgenstein, Ludwig. [1958] 1972. *Philosophical Investigations.* Trans. G.E.M. Anscombe. Oxford: Basil Blackwell. Third English edition of *Philosophische Untersuchungen,* originally published in 1967.

— 1967. *Zettel.* Ed. G.E.M. Anscombe and G.H. von Wright. Trans. G.E.M. Anscombe. Oxford. Basil Blackwell.

Woolf, Virginia. [1931] 1968. *The Waves.* Harmondsworth: Penguin.

Xenophon. [fl. 4th century BCE]. 1990. *Symposium.* In *Conversations of Socrates* [where it appears as "The Dinner Party"]. Trans. Hugh Tredennick and Robin Waterfield. Ed. Robin Waterfield. Penguin.

Yì Jīng. See *The I Ching or Book of Changes.*

Zwicky, Jan. 2015. "What Is Lyric Philosophy?" In *Alkibiades' Love: Essays in Philosophy.* Montreal: McGill-Queen's University Press, 3–18.

— 2019a. "What Is Gestalt Thinking?" In *The Experience of Meaning.* Montreal: McGill-Queen's University Press, 3–21.

— 2019b. "Simplicity and the Experience of Meaning." In *The Experience of Meaning.* Montreal: McGill-Queen's University Press, 59–74.

Index

Abram, David, 40–1
agriculture, 21–8, 126; agribiz, 26; etymology, 26; farming, 36–7, 40, 85–7
Algonquian societies, 100
Anaximander, 28
antirealism. *See* realism
Apache, Western: *godíyįhgo nagoldi'é*, 113, 126; *'ágodzaahí*, 126–7
Aristotle, 31
art, artists, 59, 68, 137–8; origin of, in Auden, 9
atrocity, 109, 115
attention, 36, 55–6, 111, 126, 130–1; failure of, 29, 35; and perception, 65; poetic, 12–13; and reverence, 40–1; as virtue, 133
Auden, W.H., 3–20, 116; poetic epistemology, 3–10, 14–20
authoritarian temperament, 141–2

Bacon, Francis, 19; Baconian science, 16–20
beauty, 15, 66, 92–3, 130; and *eros*, 138–9; moral, 104–7, 146; perception of, in Auden, 7–8; regeneration of, 146
being. *See* ontology
Bernhard, Thomas, 71–84, 159n
Berry, Wendell, 22

Bringhurst, Robert, 5, 11, 91–2
bureaucracies, 103–4, 106–7

capitalism, 24, 54, 55; origins, *vii–viii*; and postmodernism, 65; and resourcism, *viii*, 26; and 'trader' moral paradigm, 100; and Western European science, 16–17
cataclysm, ecological, *vii–viii*, 20, 88, 90–1, 93; cultural consequences, 108; documentation, 160–1nn; human complicity & denial, 90, 95, 141; pollution, 23–4; relevance of lyric thought, 117–18, 130–1; and virtue, 95–6. *See also* heat dome (2022); resourcism; technocracy
causality, causal order, 110, 113–15, 120, 127. *See also* consequence
climate, relation to weather, 88–9
climate catastrophe. *See* cataclysm, ecological
Coleridge, Samuel Taylor, 6
consequence, 119, 121; causal, 119; logical, 110, 119
consumerism. *See* pleonexia
control. *See* epistemology: of control
criteria, 18–19
culture(s): Austrian, according to

179

Thomas Bernhard, 77–8; and authoritarian temperament, 141–2; and conception of time, 125; culturing, 25–7, 125; decadence, 70; of Hapsburg Vienna, 59–63, 65; Indigenous (*see* Algonquian societies; Apache, Western; Haudenosaunee societies); and moral style, 127; Western European: disintegration, *vii–viii*, 9, 95, 108; impoverishment, 20, 56, 137. *See also* empire(s); form of life; technocracy

Dào Dé Jīng, 40, 92, 163n
death, 114, 122–3
delicacy, 15
Descartes, René, 16, 17, 31
despair, 145
Dickens, Charles, 103
Diderot, Denis, 19
discernment, 65, 107, 124, 135
Domanski, Don, 11–12, 16
Dragland, Stan, 55–6
Dù Fǔ, 143

ecology, -ies, 24, 26, 44, 63–4; of being, 132; ecological cataclysm (*see* cataclysm, ecological); of events, 120; literary, 55; moral, 99, 101; resonant ecology of world, 130
empire(s), 107, 144; collapse associated with empowerment of females, 144
Enlightenment, the, *vii*, 17, 18, 27, 121–2
epistemology, -ies, *viii*, 3; Auden's poetic epistemology, 3–10, 14–20; of control, 16–20 (*see also* technocracy); gestalt, 5, 89, 107, 123–4 (*see also* gestalt[s]); Kantian, 30–1; lineal, 120; lyric, 3, 67, 131; and moral choice, 38; oneiric, 120; Western, 18. *See also* reason, calculative
essence *vs.* accident, 66–7, 69, 113
ethics, 38, 47–57, 118, 124–8; 130, 133. *See also* beauty: moral; integrity: moral; integrity: moral and aesthetic
ethos, 112, 113, 124
evil, 146

farming. *See* agriculture
feminism, 27, 143
form of life, 63–4, 68
Freud, Sigmund, 6–7, 43, 111, 120–1
Friedell, Egon, 60, 62

gestalt(s), 44, 64; comprehension, 5, 123–4; insight, 107; intelligence, 64; intuition, 90; perception, 89; shift, 137
Ginzburg, Carlo, 90
Glubb, John, 143–4

grace, 115–16; absence of, 145
Gray, Robert, 133–4
Greene, Graham, 6
'guardian' moral paradigm, 97–100
Gustafson, Ralph, 12

Hadot, Pierre, 137–8, 140
Hass, Robert, 55
Haudenosaunee societies, 100
Havelock, Eric, 142
Haydn, Franz Joseph, 147–8
hearing-as, 5
heat dome (2022), 87, 88, 160n
Hegel, Georg Wilhelm Friedrich, 31–4, 36, 37
Heidegger, Martin, 13, 29–38, 92
Heiti, Warren, 93
Herakleitos, 43, 70, 92
Herriot, Trevor, 25
history, 31, 36, 114, 121, 135
humanities, the, 20, 135
Hume, David, 29–30, 34, 37, 81

imagination, 3, 5–6, 14; etymology, 5; Primary Imagination (Coleridge and Auden), 5–7, 9, 15, 19; Secondary Imagination (Coleridge and Auden), 5–9, 15, 19; shattered, 93
inarticulacy. *See* wordlessness
Indigenous thinkers, 40
ineffability. *See* silence; wordlessness

insight, 13, 137, 139. *See also* gestalt(s); witness
integrity, integration, 63–5, 110, 113; as ecological concept, 64; moral, 95, 126, 138; moral and aesthetic, 64–5; of world, 112, 133

Jacobs, Jane, 97–101
Joyce, James, 13
Jung, Carl, 120; archetypes, 132
justice. *See* virtues

Kafka, Franz, 103
Kant, Immanuel, 6, 29–31, 34
Keats, John, 47, 52
kingfisher, 5
Koestler, Arthur, 121
Kraus, Karl, 62–3

Lagerkvist, Pär, 116
language, 31, 33–6; as tool, 111; language-use, 7, 9, 14, 43; and lyric awareness, 11, 43, 132
Lǎo Zǐ. See *Dào Dé Jīng*
Larkin, Philip, 49, 51
law, as bulwark of liberty, 103
Lee, Dennis, 12, 15
Lǐ Bái, 132–3
Lilburn, Tim, 12, 155n
listening, 56
logic, deductive, 7, 14, 19, 30, 35, 38; and lyric, 114; species of logico-temporal consequence, 110, 112, 119, 121

Loos, Adolf, 59–62, 66, 68
Lorenz, Konrad, 40
love, 45, 92, 106, 130, 144–6; Alkibiades' for Sokrates, 138; and sorrow, 148
lyric, 68, 111–16; coherence as lyric's *eros*, 113; epistemology, 3, 67, 131; and ethics, 131, 133; form, 64, 113, 131; gesture, 110, 131; intuition, 14, 112; novels, 131; and oneiric syntax and logic, 131–2; as perception of integrated whole, 131, 133; style, 66, 68; thinkers, 42–3; thought, 117; utterance, 9

maxims, 125–8, 133
McKay, Don, 12–13, 130
meaning, 11, 65, 81–2, 84, 116; and insight, 137; meaninglessness, 82–4
Merleau-Ponty, Maurice, 40
metaphor, 44, 131; and seeing as, 5
Michaels, Anne, 13, 130
music, 5, 12, 14, 27, 117. *See also* Haydn, Franz Joseph
myth(s), 120–4, 126. *See also* Apache, Western: *godiyíhgo nagoldi'é*

narrative, 110–16, 124–5; and ethics, 118–28; etymology, 118; form, 118; syntax, 118. *See also* myth(s)
naturalist, literary, 55

nature, 44, 126, 133, 140; "end of," 23; etymology, 43–4; as female, 17; as wilderness, 23. *See also* poetry: nature
Neruda, Pablo, 109–10

ontology, 126, 144; Being in Heidegger, 34–8; as ecology, 132; and poetry, 16; nature poetry, 39–40; as synonym for 'sacred,' 10–11; ontological alienation, 43, 131; ontological applause, 13, 130; ontological astonishment, 92, 129; ontological attention, 14, 129; ontological experience, 14, 16, 144; ontological insight, 130; ontological integrity, 43, 146; ontological resonance, 19; ontological weather, 120. *See also* realism; resonance

Page, P.K., 13, 15
perception, 64–5
philosophy, 137–40; environmental, 139–40; as a way of life, 137
Plato, 92, 95–6; conception of philosophy, 139; and despair, 145–6; on *eros* for integrity, 138–9; on justice, 135–6
pleonexia, 95–6, 99–101
poet(s), poetry, 16, 29, 32, 33, 37, 117–18; nature poet(ry), 39–45, 133–4; Zen, 133

Pogue, James, 142
politics, 51–2, 95–101; epistemological, 39; and metaphysics, 67; and philosophy, 135–6, 141–4
postmodernism, 65–70
Precautionary Principle, 90–1
primary process (in Freud), 6–7, 120–1
Pythagorean theorem, 4–5, 153n

Rawls, John, 136
realism, 35, 39–40, 129–31; anti-realism, 31–5, 39–40, 62, 124; and attention, 36; lyric realism, 39–45; and moral choice, 38
reason, calculative, 14, 20. See also Bacon, Francis: Baconian science; epistemology: of control
Relations des Jésuites de la Nouvelle-France, 100
resonance, 14, 112, 117; and lyric thought, 112, 116, 117–18, 132; ontological, 19, 130; resonant order of world, 13–14, 112, 115–16, 130, 132; resonant particulars, 132
resourcism, *viii*, 25–7, 33, 91, 100. See also ontological alienation
Rilke, Rainer Maria, 15, 56, 57, 138, 155n
Rorty, Richard, 142
Rycroft, Charles, 7

sacred(ness), in Auden, 6–7, 10, 11, 15, 18–19
science, Western European, 16–19, 27, 113, 121–2; and climate change, 88; and narrative form, 113; in Kant, 29–32. See also Ginzburg, Carlo; Koestler, Arthur
secondary process (in Freud), 7
seeing as, 3–5
self, 111, 117–18; absence of sense of, 6–7, 42–3, 111–12; awareness of and capacity for tool-use, 111, 113; dissolution of, 118, 140
sequence, 110, 114, 118. See also consequence
Shelley, Percy Bysshe, 37
silence, 123, 133, 143; as healing, 42
Sinclair, Sue, 13
skepticism, 83, 137
Smailović, Vedran, 128–9
Sokrates, trial of, 142
Stenner, Karen, 141–2
Stevens, Wallace, 15
story. See myth; narrative
syntax, narrative, 110, 118–19; lineal, 120–2, 125, 126–8, 133; oneiric, 120, 122–7, 129, 131–2

technocracy, technocrat, 3, 11, 33–6, 87, 134
Thomas, Dylan, 129
time, 28; absence of sense of, 6,

115, 131; and oneiric or lineal structure, 125, 131
'trader' moral paradigm, 97–101
trust, 107
truth, 69, 113; and criteria, 18; lyric, 131; testamentary, 129–31; thinking trued by love of the real, 45

Vendler, Helen, 55
virtue(s), 95–101; attentiveness, 133; cheerfulness, 129; courage, 95–6, 98, 106; curiosity, 20, 55; empathy, *viii*, 135–6; justice, 95–6, 99, 104, 135–6; patience, 20, 27; respect, 55, 125; self-restraint, 95–6, 98; shadow virtues, 96–7; wisdom, 95–6, 98

Weil, Simone, 129, 130
Wertheimer, Max, 5, 158–9n
Western civilization. *See* culture(s), Western European
wholeness, 64, 110–11; experience or perception of, 43, 111, 123–4; as opposed to particularity, 44
wholes, 5, 13–14, 24, 66, 114; attunement to, 129; interdefinition of parts and wholes, 116, 123–4, 129; moral ecologies, 99; and particulars, 64, 132. *See also* gestalt(s); integrity; lyric; wholeness
wilderness, 13, 22–6; definition of, 24–5
witness, 115, 118, 125–30, 133; as insight, 130
Wittgenstein, Ludwig, 3, 81–2, 83, 130; in Thomas Bernhard's novels, 73, 77, 79–82
Woolf, Virginia, 56, 111–12
wordlessness, 7, 11, 14, 19, 118

Xenophon, 138
Xiè, Líng-Yùn, 41–2, 43

Yì Jīng, 120